Shakespeare's
HAMLET

LEONORA BRODWIN
ASSOCIATE PROFESSOR OF ENGLISH
ST. JOHN'S UNIVERSITY

MONARCH
PRESS

Published by
MONARCH PRESS
a Simon & Schuster division of
Gulf & Western Corporation
Simon & Schuster Building
1230 Avenue of the Americas
New York, N.Y. 10020

*MONARCH PRESS and colophon are trademarks
of Simon & Schuster, registered in the U.S. Patent
and Trademark Office.*

Standard Book Number: 0-671-00514-6

Library of Congress Catalog Card Number: 65-7242

Printed in the United States of America.

CONTENTS

INTRODUCTION:

Life of William Shakespeare **5**

Literary History of *Hamlet* **7**

Plot of *Hamlet* **8**

*DETAILED SUMMARY AND ANALYSIS
OF* HAMLET:

Act I **11**

Act II **28**

Act III **40**

Act IV **68**

Act V **85**

CHARACTER ANALYSIS **110**

SURVEY OF CRITICISM **134**

SAMPLE ESSAY QUESTIONS AND ANSWERS **143**

BIBLIOGRAPHY **152**

INTRODUCTION

LIFE OF SHAKESPEARE   In terms of mystery, the life of Shakespeare rivals that of his most celebrated creation, Hamlet. We know little more than the dates of the important events in his life that can be learned from official records. The first date is that of his christening in Holy Trinity Church, Stratford-on-Avon, on April 26, 1564. It is traditionally assumed that he was born on April 23rd of that year. His father was John Shakespeare, a tradesman of Stratford, and his mother Mary Arden, the daughter of a small landowner of Wilmcote. After filling some minor municipal posts, John Shakespeare was elected Bailiff of Stratford in 1568. William was the third child born to his parents, the eldest of four boys and two girls who survived infancy. Although there is no record of his schooling, there seems little doubt that he was educated at the free grammar school maintained by the town of Stratford which offered training in the Classical languages sufficient for university entrance.

At the age of eighteen, he married Ann Hathaway, who was eight years his senior. The license for their marriage was issued on November 27, 1582, and their first child, Susanna, was christened in Holy Trinity Church on May 26, 1583. The discrepancy between their ages plus the fact that their first child was born six months after their marriage suggests that it was a forced marriage, though this is by no means certain. At any rate, he remained with Ann for at least another two years as their additional children, the twins Hamnet and Judith, were christened on February 2, 1585. It is suggested that he left Stratford about 1585 to avoid prosecution for poaching on the property of Sir Thomas Lucy at Chalecote. After such rural beginnings he seems to have also familiarized himself with the tavern life about London, for in the plays which center about the character of Falstaff he writes of such life as from intimate acquaintance.

Whether or not he spent some time as a village schoolmaster, as tradition has it, he seems to have arrived in London about 1586 and thereafter became involved in the theatrical world through which he was to win lasting glory. The first whispers of fame occurred in 1592 when he was mentioned as an upstart playwright in Robert Greene's *Groatsworth of Wit*. The reference there is to his earliest work, the three part *Henry VI*, which probably dates from 1591. When the plague closed the London theatres during the 1593-94

5

season, Shakespeare wrote the two narrative poems, *Venus and Adonis* and *Rape of Lucrece*. Both were dedicated to the Earl of Southampton, but whether Southampton became his regular patron or enabled him to enter a more aristocratic circle we do not know. In 1594, Shakespeare became a founding member of the theatrical company known until 1603 as the Lord Chamberlain's Men and thereafter as the King's Men. Individual plays by Shakespeare began to appear in print in both honest and pirated editions, and by 1598 he was considered the leading English playwright in Francis Meres's *Paladis Tamia*. His fame as a playwright contributed heavily to the success of his company, and in 1599 the company was able to build the Globe Theatre on the south bank of the Thames to house its performances in London. But he was also active as an actor, appearing in the original performance of Ben Jonson's *Every Man in His Humour* in 1598 and *Sejanus* in 1603. Though he may have acted less in his remaining professional years, he continued as leading playwright and joint owner of the King's Men and their Globe Theatre until his retirement in 1611.

A possible sign of his rising pretensions during the early years of his success may be indicated by the fact that he secured a coat of arms for his father in 1596. This was also the year in which his son Hamnet died. By 1597 he had become so prosperous that he purchased New Place, one of the two most impressive residences in Stratford, at a cost of £60. His other large earnings were also principally invested in Stratford property. In 1601 his father died, and this is also, significantly, the year in which *Hamlet* was written. As for the rest of his family, his mother died in 1608, his daughter Susanna was married in 1607 and his daughter Judith in 1616. In 1611 he retired to live with his family at New Place in Stratford though he continued to visit London until 1614 and purchased a house in Blackfriars, London, in 1613. In March, 1616, he made a will leaving token bequests to members of his theatrical company but the bulk of his estate to his family, including the famous bequest of the second-best bed to his wife. On April 23rd (May 3rd by our calendar), 1616, he died after entertaining the playwrights Jonson and Drayton at New Place.

He was buried in the Stratford church in which he had been christened and within seven years a monument with a portrait bust was erected to his memory there. In 1623, his former fellow actors, John Hemminge and Henry Condell (both of whom had been mentioned in Shakespeare's will), edited the first complete collection of his plays, the volume known as the First Folio. The Droeshout engraving on its title page, together with the monument bust by Gerard Johnson, provide the only likenesses considered authentic. Shakespeare's wife also died in 1623 and his last surviving descendant,

Elizabeth, the daughter of Susanna, died in 1670, but the immortality of his memory has been assured by the works of his genius, so lovingly collected by his friends. The Stratford scamp who returned to his home town as its most prosperous citizen after having won fame and fortune in London honors Stratford to this day: an endless line of admirers come to pay homage before the surviving landmarks of his personal life, the house where he was born, the house in Shottery where Ann Hathaway lived, New Place, and his grave in Holy Trinity Church, before attending performances of his enduring plays.

SOURCES OF THE STORY OF HAMLET The literary history of Hamlet begins with the twelfth-century *Historia Danica* of Saxo Grammaticus which recounts the legendary history of "Amlethus." Printed in 1514, it was freely adapted into French in the fifth volume of François de Belleforest's *Histoires Tragiques,* published in 1576. That there was also a play about Hamlet on the English stage by 1589, possibly written by Thomas Kyd, is suggested in Thomas Nashe's epistle to Robert Greene's *Menaphon,* published in that year. A performance of this older version of *Hamlet,* referred to in modern scholarship as the *Ur-Hamlet,* is recorded for 1594, but the play itself is lost.

EARLY TEXTUAL HISTORY OF SHAKESPEARE'S HAMLET Basing his story largely upon the account in Belleforest, Shakespeare's version of *Hamlet* was written in 1601. Its success was so immediate that a pirated version, the so-called "bad-quarto," was published in 1603. The corruption and brevity of this text were so great as to necessitate the publication of an authentic copy of the play in 1604-5. This so-called "good-quarto" or, more technically, the Second Quarto, is almost double the length of the "bad quarto" and is thought to have been printed from Shakespeare's own copy of the play. The third printed version of Shakespeare's play, that in the 1623 folio, is thought to have been printed from the prompt-book of Shakespeare's acting company. The Second Quarto is generally regarded as the best text but most modern editors collate it with the variants in the First Folio edition for their modern texts of the play. The Act, Scene and Line references which are universally used today derive from the work of nineteenth century editors, as the quarto texts were undivided and the folio text almost so. Though these divisions are not Shakespeare's own, they are used today to facilitate easy reference.

TRADITION OF REVENGE TRAGEDY The tradition of revenge tragedy dates back to the Classical Greek drama and in particular to the *Oresteia* of Aeschylus, but it was through the Latin plays of Seneca, particularly *Thyestes,* that the form became popular, first in the universities and law schools and then in the professional theatres of England. The first extant English revenge tragedy and also one of the earliest of any extant English tragedies was *The Spanish Tragedy* by Thomas Kyd, written about 1589. Although this tragedy began with the figure of a ghost calling for revenge and involved the madness of one of its principal characters, it has otherwise little connection with Shakespeare's *Hamlet*. Had we the lost *Hamlet*, which Kyd may have also authored, we would be able to see more easily the English dramatic traditions on which Shakespeare built. We are fortunate in this regard, however, to have the next important revenge tragedy, John Marston's *Antonio's Revenge*, the second part of the two part play entitled *Antonio and Mellida*, which was written in 1599.

A COMPARISON OF ANTONIO AND HAMLET　　In the character of Antonio, which may have been derived from Kyd's (?) *Hamlet*, we may trace the outlines of the character of Shakespeare's *Hamlet*. In love with Mellida, Antonio is the son of the King deposed by her usurping father, Piero. Piero is a Machiavellian villain who seems to agree to their marriage, but then opposes it on the falsified grounds of his daughter's unfaithful lust. Antonio assumes the role of court fool and has it given out that Antonio has drowned himself for love of Mellida. This breaks her heart and she dies. In a state of extreme depression over Mellida's death and Piero's pursuit of his mother, Antonio visits his father's tomb where his cries of suicidal anguish raise up his father's ghost who lays upon him the duty of revenge. In pursuit of this revenge his sensitive spirit becomes so warped that he viciously kills Piero's innocent little son, Julio, who loves Antonio. When he finally accomplishes his brutal revenge, Marston permits him to continue to live in religious retirement. Both Antonio and Hamlet have sensitive spirits which are warped by the evils surrounding them. Both of their fathers have lost their thrones; both of their mothers are loved by the rulers who have taken their fathers' places; both of their own romances are curtailed through the influence of a corrupt court; both are suicidally depressed before and after they have been given the duty of revenge; both assume the guise of madmen; both inflict as great injury as they have received, and both are finally vindicated by their authors. The type of the Revenger—warped by the sufferings of his sensitive spirit but exonerated, nonetheless, by his artistic creator—had already been shaped by Marston when Shakespeare turned his hand to the subject of Hamlet. What Shakespeare did to the character of his Revenger was to endow his perception with genius and place him in a context of mystery.

THE PLOT　　A sense of mystery permeates the plot beginning with the mysterious appearance of the ghost. Hamlet is first shown in suicidal despair over the death of his father and hasty remarriage of his mother to her brother-in-law and the new King of Denmark, Claudius. Brought to meet the apparent ghost of his father, Hamlet pledges to revenge his murder by Claudius who, the ghost also informs Hamlet, had already committed adultery with his Queen during his lifetime. Though Hamlet accepts the ghost's word while he is with him, seeds of doubt about the ghost's authenticity have been sown from the very beginning of the play and continue to torment Hamlet for much of its remainder. For it may be that the figure of the ghost is actually a diabolic impersonation of the spirit of Hamlet's father come to tempt him to his damnation. The better to investigate Claudius' guilt, Hamlet assumes the guise of madness, though the sight of his father's spirit has caused his already unstable spirit to totter on the brink of actual insanity. This combination of real and assumed mental instability results in so worrying Claudius that he begins to spy on Hamlet in turn to try to understand whether Hamlet represents a danger to him. He first sets Rosencrantz and Guildenstern to spy on Hamlet and then spies upon a prearranged meeting between Hamlet and his estranged sweetheart, Ophelia. Meanwhile, Hamlet has thought of a new means to test Claudius' guilt and the authenticity of the ghost; he will stage a performance of a play which will reproduce Claudius' crime and observe his reaction to it. This plan is successful as Claudius breaks down during the performance but, since the performance also alerts Claudius to Hamlet's knowledge of his crime and consequent danger to him, he also acts to exile Hamlet to England. His chief advisor, Polonius, prevails upon Claudius to permit one final spying attempt upon Hamlet before he is exiled; his mother is to call Hamlet to her room, where Polonius will be hidden to overhear the conference, and prevail upon him to confide in her.

For the two months since Hamlet had seen the ghost, Hamlet has been mysteriously unable to commit his vowed revenge. Unable to explain to himself either his long delay or his generally depressed condition, he has investigated this problem as eagerly as Claudius and Polonius. He had first rationalized his delay on the grounds of doubt about the ghost's nature. But after Claudius's breakdown during the performance of the play clears Hamlet's mind of this doubt, he has an immediate opportunity for revenge when he accidentally comes upon the guilt-ridden Claudius alone in prayer. Again he rationalizes himself into delay, this time on the grounds that his revenge would not be horrible enough as Claudius's penitence might save his soul from hell. He goes to his mother's room, but in such an unnaturally excited state that he scares his mother and the hidden Polonius into crying for help. His enraged murderous impulse, restrained from releasing itself upon Claudius or upon his mother, madly lashes out at the hidden figure and results in the death of Polonius. This unpremeditated act seals Hamlet's own doom.

The first effect of this rash act is to cause Claudius to alter his order for Hamlet's exile so that he will be executed in England. While on shipboard to England, however, Hamlet again acts rashly; he discovers the letter ordering his death and changes it so that the bearers, Rosencrantz and Guildenstern, will be put to death in his place. His success in this rash enterprise leads him to the religious perception that "There's a divinity that shapes our ends,/ Rough-hew them how we wlil." Escaping from the ship during an attack upon it by pirates, he returns to Denmark with a clear conscience both about his coming revenge against Claudius and his own order for the executions of Rosencrantz and Guildenstern. But he makes no plans for his revenge since he has come to place his full confidence upon Providence. This is not true, however, of Claudius or of Laertes, the son of Polonius, who has also returned to Denmark to revenge his own father's death. Forewarned by Hamlet of his return, they lay plans for his death through a fencing match in which Laertes will use an illegally sharp and poisoned sword backed up by a poisoned drink. Laertes' grievance against Hamlet is increased by the madness and death of his sister, Ophelia, and by Hamlet's aggressive behavior towards him when they meet at her funeral. But the plans of Claudius and Laertes backfire with the result that both they and Hamlet's mother are killed in addition to Hamlet. At the cost of his own life, Hamlet has, however, achieved his revenge in terms that exonerate his soul from the danger of damnation into which Claudius seems to be sunk. Celebrated for his nobility of spirit he is finally given a hero's funeral.

BRIEF NOTE ON THE CRITICISM   Hamlet's mysterious delay in fulfilling his revenge has led to much critical speculation about the so-called "problem of Hamlet." From Goethe and Coleridge to Freud and his disciples, much theorizing has been done on the mysterious factor in Hamlet's character which inhibits him from taking this action. But more recently this question has been placed in the larger context of the whole play's mysterious quality, the various investigations of the characters being seen to point to the deeper mystery of reality which is concentrated in the mysterious figure of the ghost and the ironic workings of Providence. *Hamlet* has come to be viewed not simply as the psychological tragedy of its hero but as profound religious drama which attempts to explore as well the cosmic mysteries of existence. At the beginning of the tragedy Hamlet tells his skeptical friend: "There are more things in heaven and earth, Horatio,/ Than are dreamt of in your philosophy." In the coming analysis of the action of the play and its characters we shall try to unravel of these mysteries, but of others we must stand in awe before Shakespeare's genius and the profundity of his creation.

ACT I: SCENE 1

The play opens at a sentry post before the castle of Elsinore, Denmark, during legendary times. It is midnight and Francisco, a sentry, is at his post awaiting his relief. Bernardo enters and asks, "Who's there?" But Francisco challenges him for the password, saying, "Nay, answer me; stand, and unfold yourself."

> **COMMENT:** These opening two lines are significant for they set a tone of watchful suspicion which is later to characterize the major characters and their supporters: Hamlet, with the aid of Horatio, spies on Claudius, while Claudius, with the aid of Rosencrantz, Guildenstern, Polonius, Ophelia and Gertrude, spies on Hamlet; on a minor level, Polonius also spies on his son Laertes.

Horatio and Marcellus, who are to share Bernardo's sentry duty this evening, now enter. Horatio is not a regular sentry but has been especially asked by Marcellus to spend this watch with them because of something unusual which has occurred on the two previous nights for which they wish his opinion and help. When Bernardo greets Horatio with the question whether it really is he, Horatio replies, "A piece of him." Marcellus now tells Bernardo that Horatio has rejected their story as "fantasy" and will not allow himself to believe it.

> **COMMENT:** These few remarks help to define the character of Horatio. We later learn that Horatio is a Stoic, a follower of an ancient Greek and Roman philosophy which held that the pain of life could be overcome by the suppression of all personal desire, by remaining equally unmoved by joy or grief, and by submitting without complaint to what was unavoidable. Since a person who has suppressed all of his emotional reactions might be said to be living on only a partial level, Horatio has well replied that all that is present is "a piece of him." The other aspect of Horatio's character which is here suggested is his skeptical turn of mind, his refusal to accept superstitious hearsay evidence and also, as we shall later learn, his avoidance of the deeper mysteries of life.

Marcellus proceeds to explain the "dreaded sight" that has appeared before them the last two nights, but, before he and Bernardo have half begun their tale, the Ghost enters. Horatio agrees with the two sentries that the Ghost, who is dressed in armor, has a form like that of the dead King Hamlet. Marcellus suggests that, since Horatio is a "scholar," he should be the one to know how to speak to the Ghost. Horatio does this, beginning by asking the Ghost, "What art thou?" and closing with the challenge, "by heaven I charge thee, speak!" But Marcellus notes that "It is offended," and Bernardo that "it stalks away." Now that his own eyes have seen the Ghost, Horatio admits that it is "something more than fantasy" and that it forbodes "some strange eruption to our state," some coming disaster.

Marcellus now asks Horatio whether he knows why there is such a strict watch and why the country is so busy building armaments. Horatio replies that, as they know, the late King Fortinbras of Norway, jealous of the martial conquests of the late Danish King Hamlet, challenged the Danish King to combat, staking all his possessions on the outcome, and that the late Hamlet killed Fortinbras and took over his forfeited lands as had been agreed. Recently, however, young Fortinbras, son of the slain King, had raised an unlawful army with the apparent aim to recover by force of arms the territories his father had lost to the Danes. It is against such a possibility, Horatio thinks, that the present Danish military preparations have been undertaken. Bernardo agrees with this and further suggests that it may be in connection with these wars, with which the late King Hamlet is still so involved, that his Ghost has now been aroused. Horatio is not so sure of this as he is troubled by the remembrance of similar supernatural occurrences before the murder of Julius Caesar: ghosts in the Roman streets, comets, bloody dews, ominous signs in the sun, and a lengthy eclipse of the moon. He suggests that "heaven and earth" are demonstrating a similar "omen" to "feared events" for their own country.

COMMENT: Shakespeare had placed much importance on these supernatural occurrences in his earlier tragedy, *Julius Caesar,* and is to use the supernatural prophetic figures of the witches in his later tragedy, *Macbeth.* This suggests that Shakespeare is using these supernatural appearances not only to thrill and amaze the "groundlings" (the poor, uneducated part of the audience that stood on the ground before the stage to watch the performance), although he is certainly using these figures with great dramatic effectiveness, but also to suggest something about reality, namely that the whole of the universe is involved in and disrupted by human evil and will work in mysterious ways to right the balance of nature.

At this point the Ghost re-enters and Horatio, recognizing the danger involved, vows to cross it even if it destroys him. He challenges the Ghost to speak to him, but only on certain conditions. He first proposes "If there be any good thing to be done/That may to thee do ease and grace to me,/Speak to me." The second condition under which Horatio will permit the Ghost to speak to him is if he has some secret knowledge of his country's fate which his country might avoid by being told of it; and the third condition is if the Ghost wishes to reveal the hiding place of any treasure he may have buried. Before the Ghost can answer, however, the cock crows and, as the three characters try vainly with their swords to force the Ghost to stand and answer the questions, the Ghost fades away. Horatio notes that he has often heard that at the cock's warning of the approach of day the "erring spirit" must return "to his confine" and that the present disappearance of the Ghost seems to confirm the truth of this saying. Marcellus agrees, but further notes that there are those who say that at the Christmas season,

> Wherein our Saviour's birth is celebrated,
> The cock crows all night long.
> And then, they say, no spirit dare stir abroad,
> The nights are wholesome, then no planets strike,
> No fairy takes, nor witch hath power to charm.
> So hallowed and so gracious is that time.

COMMENT: From the last speech there would seem to be some opposition between the religion of Christ and such supernatural manifestations as were earlier discussed, ghosts, fairies, witches and planetary disturbances. Furthermore, we have seen that Horatio was very careful, in confronting the ghost, to guard himself against any evil power it might possess. In his first confrontation, he charged the ghost to disclose his true nature and to speak to him "by heaven." In his second confrontation, he charges the ghost only to speak to him if he wishes him to do a good thing which will bring him grace. Horatio's behavior suggests the morally questionable nature of the ghost and serves as a Christian model against which Hamlet's later confrontation with the ghost may be judged.

As it is now morning, Horatio suggests that they break up their watch and go to Hamlet to tell him what they have seen, for he suspects that "This spirit, dumb to us, will speak to him." Marcellus agrees and they depart from the stage.

SUMMARY This opening scene has the following important
purposes:

1. It serves as an "exposition," a setting forth of the important
   occurrences which precede the beginning of the play: the war
   between Norway and Denmark which was won by the late King
   Hamlet, young Fortinbras' military preparations to regain Norway's lost territories, and Denmark's counter military
   preparations.

2. It provides an exciting and suspenseful beginning to the play
   through the introduction of the ominous and silent ghost who
   is, in fact, going to motivate the action of the entire play.

3. It raises some questions as to the nature and importance of
   supernatural manifestations in general and of this ghost in
   particular and also questions the relation of such manifestations to Christianity, questions which will be raised repeatedly
   throughout the play.

4. It introduces us to the character of Horatio, a skeptical Stoic,
   who is to become Hamlet's one close friend and in relation to
   whom we may be the better judge Hamlet.

ACT I: SCENE 2

The second scene opens on the following day with the entrance of
King Claudius and the important members of his court into a room
of state in the castle at Elsinore. Claudius begins the scene with a
formal public address to his court which touches on the important
matters of state before him.

The first item which Claudius takes up is his hasty marriage to his
brother's widow, Queen Gertrude. He explains that, as she has an
equal right to the throne and as his own desires also favored her, he
has married her even though it is less than two months since the
death of her husband and his brother, the late King Hamlet. He
admits that it might have ben more fitting for him and the whole
kingdom to remain in mourning for the late King rather than to
celebrate a marriage, but he states that he has only proceeded in
this matter because his chief counselors of state had freely advised
him to do so, for, which he thanks them.

The second item of state, and the real reason for this meeting, is
concerned with the activities of young Fortinbras, of which we

have already learned something in the first scene. We are now told that Fortinbras, believing Denmark to be disorganized and weak as a result of the death of King Hamlet, had sent several messages to Claudius demanding the surrender of the lands lost by his father. Claudius' response is to send an envoy to the King of Norway, the uncle of young Fortinbras, who, old and bedridden, has scarcely heard of the unlawful activities of his nephew. In the letter he is sending to the King of Norway, Claudius demands that he suppress the unlawful activities of his nephew, further suggesting that the cost of rearming Norway is all coming out of the King of Norway's own revenues and that he had better look into this matter. Claudius now dispatches Cornelius and Voltemand to carry this letter to the King of Norway as quickly as possible.

The third item is the personal request of Laertes, son of the Lord Chamberlain, Polonius, to be permitted to return to Paris, from which he had come to attend Claudius' coronation. Before Claudius allows Laertes to make his request, he tells him how willing he is to grant him any request because of the great respect the throne of Denmark holds for his father. Upon learning the nature of the request, he refers the decision to Polonius, who gives his consent to his son's leaving, which is then seconded by Claudius.

COMMENT: The style of Claudius' opening speech is majestic, balanced and controlled, indicating similar qualities in his character. These qualities may help to explain why he was elected to the throne of Denmark over the pretensions of his nephew, Hamlet, son to the late King Hamlet (for the king of Denmark was elected to the throne by the nobility from among the members of the royal family). His imposing statesmanship is further indicated by his activities since gaining the throne, as shown in this speech. He has only fulfilled his personal desire to marry Gertrude after gaining the cooperation and support of his chief counselors, one of whom, Polonius, we here see him treating with exaggerated marks of deference. Claudius, then, appears to be an able politician with regards to members of his own court. But, more than this, he is also a statesman. Although preparing for war, as we have learned from Horatio in the first scene, he prefers to avoid war if it is possible to do so through diplomatic means, and, as we shall later learn, his letter to the King of Norway is successful in accomplishing this purpose. Fortinbras' conjectures as to the weak and disorganized state of Denmark are seen to be completely false as Claudius, in less than two months of rule, has ably taken the situation in hand.

Claudius now turns to the last item of business, the desire of his nephew, now step-son, Hamlet, to return to his studies in Wittenberg. But, as Claudius addresses him with the words "my cousin Hamlet, and my son," Hamlet says to himself, "A little more than kin, and less than kind!"

COMMENT: In this first silent speech (called an "aside" in the stage directions) of Hamlet, we learn something of the quality of his mind. For what Hamlet is doing is making a bitter little joke to himself. This joke is based upon a pun on the meanings of the word "kind." Originally, and still in the seventeenth century when *Hamlet* was written, the word "kind" meant that which naturally pertains to "kindred," especially those feelings of care and concern, "kindness," which blood relations should feel for each other. When Hamlet uses the word "kind," then, he is referring to both "kindness" in our sense of the term and "kinship." Claudius, then is "a little more than kin," than that second degree of relationship indicated generally by the term "cousin" since he is now also his step-father, but he is also a little less than kin, in the older sense of the term "kind," an apparent paradox which is resolved by the other meaning of "kind," namely, the "kindness" associated with blood relations. This bitter joke, made for his own amusement, conveys Hamlet's suspicions regarding Claudius' integrity: first, that though Claudius may be acting with a show of kindred concern, his feelings for him are far from fatherly, and secondly and more vaguely, that his feelings for Hamlet's true father may have been far from brotherly, though how far Hamlet does not dare suggest even to himself. Since such suspicions would be serious, indeed, if valid, Hamlet is protecting himself from the full weight of his suspicions through the use of humor, though it is humor of a very biting variety.

Claudius now asks Hamlet how it is that he is still in such a downcast state of mourning, and Hamlet quickly retorts that his mourning is not sufficient. His mother begs him to put off his mourning attire and gloom and look with more friendliness upon Claudius, to seek in him rather than in the dust for his father, and, finally, to accept the fact of his natural father's death since he knows " 'tis common. All that lives must die." Hamlet agrees: "Ay madam, it is common." Gertrude next asks why it then "seems" so special to him, not understanding that the very commonness of death may increase rather than diminish Hamlet's despair. Hamlet picks up her innocent use of the word "seems" to disclaim any such false appearance: "Seems, madam? Nay, it is. I know not 'seems'." His full mourning is not simply an outward show which a man might play since his inner feelings go beyond all such external appearances: "I have that within which passeth show." Claudius says that it is good for a son to give such mourning duties to his father as long as it is held to some prescribed term but that to continue beyond such a time is impious and unmanly; "It shows a will most incorrect to heaven" since it stubbornly refuses to accept the will of heaven. Claudius begs Hamlet to put aside his mourning, to think of him as his father for he does feel towards Hamlet as a father, and to make him happy by remaining beside him in Denmark rather than returning to Wittenberg. The Queen seconds this desire on her own account and Hamlet replies that he will obey her. Claudius is so delighted with this unforced reply that he vows to spend the evening toasting Hamlet's apparent reconciliation with him. With this, the formal audience is over and the King and court depart from the stage, leaving Hamlet alone.

We have now arrived at Hamlet's first "soliloquy," a term for the Elizabethan stage convention which permits a character to speak directly to the audience his inner, silent thoughts. Hamlet begins with the anguished wish that his "solid" (some scholars, following Kittredge, would substitute "sullied" here as the word Shakespeare originally intended) "flesh would melt" away by itself. Since this cannot be, he wishes that God had not given a direct law forbidding suicide. He continues with an anguished general cry against the will of heaven: "O God, God, / How weary, stale, flat, and unprofitable / Seem to me all the uses of this world!" He is led to this cry of despair by his recent recognition that justice does not rule the world, that "things rank and gross in nature possess it merely." The world appears to him in this light because his "excellent" father has died and Claudius, so far inferior to his father, has succeeded to his place, not only to his father's throne but also to his wife. But it is his mother's behavior which has most disillusioned him. His father had been "so loving" and gentle to his mother and she had seemed to return his affection, "would hang on him" as if the more she was with him the more her "appetite" for him would grow. (Note that Hamlet expresses his father's feelings for his mother as "love" but his mother's feelings for his father as "appetite," a sign of his new awareness of the "grossness" of nature in general and of his mother in particular.) Not only that, she had seemed genuinely overcome by grief at his father's funeral. "And yet within a month" she had married. The thought is so horrifying to him that he tries to close it out from his mind, "Let me not think on't," for as soon as he does think of it he must condemn his mother and, with her, all women: "frailty, thy name is woman." (The fact that the happy marriage of his parents, in which he had believed all of his life, now seems to have been a delusion—that his mother could not have loved his father as much as she appeared

to since she now acts the same way with another man, and that
man her brother-in-law—shows Hamlet that he did not know the
true nature of the person closest to him, his mother, and that,
if he cannot even trust his own mother, there is no one he may
trust. In the past two months, then, two terrible facts of human
existence have been brought personally home to him through his
loved ones: the fact of death and the fact of human imperfection
and falseness, and these have so disillusioned him with the value
of life that he has sunk completely into a suicidal state of mind.)
He is particularly heartbroken over the behavior of his mother and
over the fact that there is nothing he can do about it: "It is not,
nor it cannot come to good./But break my heart, for I must hold
my tongue."

At this point Horatio enters with Marcellus and Bernardo. Hamlet
quickly rouses himself from his suicidal reflections and is delighted
to see Horatio, a fellow student of his at the University of Wittenberg whom he holds in high respect. Asked what he is doing in
Elsinore, Horatio, who for some unexplained reason has not pre-
viously greeted Hamlet, replies that "I came to see your father's
funeral." Hamlet ironically returns: "do not mock me fellow
student./I think it was to see my mother's wedding." When Horatio
agrees that it followed quickly upon the funeral, Hamlet replies
with further satiric bite: "Thrift, thrift, Horatio The funeral baked
meats/Did coldly furnish forth the marriage tables." And then he
more seriously expresses his displeasure.

COMMENT: In the past scene we have seen rapid shifts in
Hamlet's moods. First he reflects satirically to himself on the
nature of Claudius; then he expresses himself in a melancholy
fashion to his mother on the subject of his continuing mourning; thirdly, he reflects in a melancholy fashion to himself on
his desire for suicide as a result of his mother's remarriage;
lastly, he expresses himself satirically to Horatio, also on the
subject of his mother's remarriage. We see, first, that he does
not express himself differently to himself from the way he does
to others; he is both satiric and melancholy to himself and
both satiric and melancholy to others, depending upon his
particular mood at the moment. Secondly, we see that he
alternates only between these two moods, moods that have a
special relationship to one another.

Satire is a particularly destructive form of wit, as is indicated
by such an expression as a "satiric thrust," but it achieves
its destructive purpose through humiliating laughter. If satire
directs a destructive mood outwards, even though only
through laughter, melancholy is, in its extreme form, a sui-

cidal, self-destructive mood. Both are responses to a similar vision of the tormenting imperfections of life; in the former case the desire is to destroy the imperfections of life; in the latter to destroy the self because it can no longer endure these imperfections. But whether directed with murderous or suicidal intent, this destructive impulse shows, in Claudius' words, "a will most incorrect to heaven," for both of these desires are equally forbidden by religious law, as Hamlet is aware in his first soliloquy; he is forbidden to commit suicide and he must hold his tongue. Since death is so common that it expresses the will of heaven, Claudius asks Hamlet: "Why should we in our peevish opposition/Take it to heart?" But this is exactly Hamlet's condition; the evil in the universe has suddenly come home to him and he does "take it to heart." He cannot accept the will of heaven in this regard and yet, as he will not actively oppose God, his opposition is reduced to frustrated peevishness which expresses itself in alternating moods of satire and melancholy.

Horatio now tells Hamlet that a ghost with the appearance of his father has three times appeared before the midnight sentries at their guard post and that he had been present at the last visitation. Hamlet questions Horatio minutely as to the appearance of the spirit and, convinced of its similarity to his father, resolves to appear at the watch that night. He vows: "If it assume my noble father's person,/I'll speak to it though hell itself should gape."

COMMENT: At the time when *Hamlet* was written, rather than in the legendary time in which it was set, the University of Wittenberg was a center of Protestant theology. With historical inconsistency, Shakespeare casts his legendary character, Hamlet, as a student at a contemporary university. As a student at Wittenberg, Hamlet would have been taught the orthodox Protestant position on ghosts which was that they were not the spirits of the deceased but either angels or, what was far more general, devils who "assumed" the appearance of a deceased person to tempt a surviving relative into spiritual damnation. Whereas Horatio had originally accepted the more extreme, skeptical position that ghosts do not exist, Hamlet approaches his coming meeting with the ghost with the belief that it is probably a devil who has "assumed" his father's form in order to damn him to hell. But he is willing to risk this danger to learn the ghost's message.

Hamlet asks the guards to tell no one of the appearance of the ghost, saying that he will reward them for their silence, and, appointing a meeting for that night, bids them farewell. They leave and, alone, Hamlet expresses his suspicion that there has been "some foul play," a reechoing of his earlier, half thought suspicion.

SUMMARY   This scene accomplishes the following purposes:

1. It serves as an introduction to the play's two leading characters, Claudius and Hamlet, whom Hamlet is later to call "mighty opposites." Claudius is presented as immensely capable of dealing with the problems of state and of life; he has established an ordered, efficient state and diplomatically avoids war, and he preaches to Hamlet the acceptance of life with all its evils. Hamlet is shown to be a brilliant, sensitive, highly erratic and moody person who refuses to accept the imperfections of life and has been driven into a suicidal frame of mind by the death of his father and infidelity of his mother.

2. By the end of the scene, Hamlet, despite his personal withdrawal, has become involved in the action. He has complied with the request of Claudius and his mother that he remain at the Danish court rather than return to Wittenberg as he had desired, and he has resolved to speak with the ghost and learn its bidding even though it damn him (further indication of the uncertain nature of the ghost).

ACT I: SCENE 3

The scene is set in Polonius' rooms within the castle at Elsinore later that day. Laertes is about to leave for Paris and is bidding his sister, Ophelia, farewell. In a long speech, he warns her not to trust Hamlet's intentions towards her and to protect her chastity, for even though Hamlet may say he loves her and perhaps now does, he cannot marry as he wishes since he is of royal birth and is thus far above her. She answers that she will follow his advice but that he should not simply preach strictness to her and then act like a libertine himself. At this point Polonius enters surprised that Laertes is still there since the wind is up and he is waited for at the boat. He hurries him to go, gives him his blessing, and then delays his departure with moral commonplaces: he should be discreet in words and action; devote himself to true friends rather than every new acquaintance; avoid quarrels but, once involved, bear himself strongly; listen to all but reserve his true thoughts only to a few; accept other men's criticism but refrain from criticizing others; dress with an elegance that is not gaudy, for appearance is often used as a guide to the nature of a man; neither borrow nor lend; "This above all, to thine own self be true,/And it must follow as the night the day/Thou canst not then be false to any man."

> **COMMENT:** We see that Laertes takes after his father in long-winded, moral preaching. Polonius, in fact, appears foolish in this regard. He comes out, hurrying Laertes to leave, "Yet here, Laertes? Aboard, aboard, for shame!" And yet he delays him with standard moralizing. That this extremely well written speech does not reflect the wise fruits of a lifetime of reflection, as it is often held to do, is shown by the fact that, although he claims integrity to be the most important moral quality, he is himself the falsest of men, as we shall later see.

Laertes now leaves, bidding Ophelia to "remember well what I have said to you." Polonius questions Ophelia as to what this is and is told that it concerns Hamlet. This reminds Polonius that he has been told of the meetings between Hamlet and Ophelia and asks her what there is between them. To her reply that Hamlet has recently given her many signs of his "affection", Polonius expresses disgust: "Affection? Pooh!" He tells her that she is just an innocent girl if she believes Hamlet's intentions. When she says that he has spoken to her of "love in honorable fashion," Polonius says that this is just a trap to seduce her. To protect his daughter's honor and his own, he tells her first that she should not see Hamlet so often, in fact, should play harder to get. But as he continues to explain the ways of men to his innocent daughter, he becomes more and more convinced of her danger until he suddenly decides that she must not see him again and so commands her. She is an obedient daughter and agrees to obey him, at which they leave the stage.

> **COMMENT:** Polonius' lack of true wisdom, earlier suggested, is here confirmed. He does not investigate the nature of Hamlet's intentions but assumes that they must be dishonorable and that a marriage between the prince and his daughter would be impossible. We later learn that he was wrong on both counts as, at Ophelia's funeral, Gertrude says that she had hoped Ophelia would be Hamlet's wife and Hamlet proclaims his love for her. Furthermore, his sudden decision not to permit his daughter to see Hamlet again, a decision arrived at without any considered judgment, is a serious error, as he later admits, since it serves to reinforce Hamlet's disillusionment with women which, in turn, helps to break Ophelia's heart and destroy her sanity. In his relations to his daughter, then, he shows an overbearing authority and apparent worldly wisdom without true discretion.

SUMMARY　This scene serves the following purposes:

1. It introduces us more fully to the important character of Polonius and shows him to be a foolish, authoritarian old man, verging on senility. His foolish self-importance, which is even more fully revealed later on, causes him to be treated in many instances as a comic character. But his effects and end are far from comic.

2. It also introduces us to Ophelia, an innocent, obedient young girl, and to the fact of Hamlet's love for her.

3. The action of the scene is important in so far as Polonius' decision to restrict his daughter from seeing Hamlet bars Hamlet's love from any normal development it might have had, and also seriously hurts Ophelia.

ACT I: SCENES 4 AND 5

Hamlet, Horatio and Marcellus enter the platform before the castle where the sentry post is situated. It is midnight, as they note, and some trumpets are heard to sound. Horatio asks Hamlet what it means and Hamlet replies that the King and court are spending the evening drinking and that every time Claudius makes a toast, the trumpets and drums sound. Horatio asks whether this is a Danish custom and Hamlet says that it is, but that though he is a native here "and to the manner born," he thinks it better not to keep this time-honored custom which has given Denmark a reputation for drunkenness among other nations.

> **COMMENT:**　In Scene 2, Claudius had referred to his habitual evening drinking when he said that once "again" he would make loud toasts with wine that evening in honor of his reconciliation with Hamlet. When Hamlet greeted Horatio he said to him: "We'll teach you to drink deep ere you depart." Here we see another difference between Claudius and Hamlet; Claudius indulges in sensual pleasure while Hamlet views such indulgence with puritanical disgust.

Hamlet continues that, just as Denmark's positive achievements are overshadowed by its reputation for drunkenness, so it can happen in the case of particular men. A personality defect with which they are born, and for which they cannot be held guilty, may so develop that it leads to irrational behavior, or a habit may similarly overcome the control of their reason. Then such men, carrying "the

stamp of one defect," though they have all other virtues, will come
under general condemnation for this one fault.

>   **COMMENT:** This has generally been taken to represent
>   Shakespeare's discussion of the concept of the "tragic flaw."
>   This concept holds that the proper tragic hero is one who is
>   above average in virtue but is brought to tragedy as a result
>   of one flaw in his character. The concept is generally thought
>   to be derived from Aristotle's *Poetics* but is actually a Renais-
>   sance interpretation of Aristotle. In any case, critics are in
>   greater agreement about the meaning of this passage than
>   about the nature of Hamlet's supposed "tragic flaw."

At this point the ghost enters. Hamlet calls upon the angels to defend him and then addresses the ghost. He says that whether he is
an angel come from heaven with charitable intent, or a damned
spirit come from hell with wicked intent (the only two possibilities
he considers), the question is so uncertain that he will speak to him
as though he were the true spirit of his father. He asks him why
he has returned from death, but the ghost, rather than answer him,
silently beckons Hamlet to follow him. Horatio and Marcellus
advise Hamlet not to follow the ghost, but Hamlet says he has
nothing to fear since "I do not set my life at a pin's fee." Horatio
says that the ghost might tempt him to the edge of the cliff, drive
him mad, and then cause him to commit suicide (possibilities which
might follow if the ghost were a devil). But Hamlet answers, "My
fate cries out," and, breaking away from Horatio and Marcellus
who are now physically holding him back, he follows the ghost to
another part of the platform, leaving the stage. Though Marcellus
now says, "Something is rotten in the state of Denmark," Horatio
hopes the coming of the ghost may have a blessed effect. He says,
"Heaven will direct it." In any case, they decide it is not fit to leave
Hamlet alone and follow him.

The fifth scene begins with the entrance of the ghost on another
part of the platform. Hamlet follows but then tells the ghost to
stop and speak because he will follow him no further. The ghost
turns and now finally reveals that he is the true spirit of Hamlet's
father, doomed for a certain term to purgatory; he has returned to
earth to tell Hamlet that if he ever loved his father he should
"Revenge his foul and most unnatural murder."

>   **COMMENT:** Up to this point we have noted three dif-
>   ferent attitudes towards ghosts: Marcellus' superstitious be-
>   lief in the existence of ghosts without too much certainty as to
>   their nature; Horatio's initial disbelief in the existence of
>   ghosts; and Hamlet's Protestant belief that ghosts are the ap-

pearance of either angels or devils in the assumed form of a deceased person. Now we see the fourth possible Renaissance attitude towards ghosts, the Catholic position that ghosts are the true spirits of deceased persons who are in purgatory. This is the position the ghost holds of himself, though this does not necessarily mean that he is telling Hamlet the truth.

Whatever be the truth of the matter (and the doubt is to continue to torment Hamlet), the ghost is acting in a way traditional for ghosts since pre-Christian, Classical times—he is calling for revenge. There is a whole tradition of revenge tragedy dating from ancient Greece and Rome and continuing in plays in the Elizabethan drama before *Hamlet* in which a ghost appears calling for revenge and establishes the motive for the tragic action. The difference between Classical and Christian tragedy, however, is that in the latter the ghost's demand for revenge conflicts with the Christian commandment against murder. This fact serves to reinforce the possible identification of the ghost with the devil since his demand would lead to damnation in Christian terms. (For a fuller discussion of the subject of the ghost, see John Dover Wilson's *What Happens in Hamlet,* to which the present treatment is much indebted).

Upon learning of his father's murder, Hamlet is anxious to learn the name of his murderer that he may be "swift" in his revenge. But when the ghost reveals that the murderer is Claudius, Hamlet exclaims, "O my prophetic soul!" (This indicates that Hamlet had dimly suspected as much, as was earlier shown.) The ghost now reveals something else, that Claudius had seduced his "most seeming-virtuous queen" to "shameful lust" before his death. And the ghost agrees with Hamlet as to the relative merits of Claudius and himself when he says: "O Hamlet, what a falling-off was there." Though he considers Claudius "a wretch whose natural gifts were poor to those of mine," he also understands that lust will leave "a radiant angel" to "prey on garbage." He then explains how he was killed, that he was sleeping in his orchard in the afternoon when Claudius poured poison in his ear which quickly killed him. "Most horrible" of all, Claudius' murder deprived him of the opportunity of confession and of the Sacraments before death. He now tells Hamlet that if he has any natural feeling for his father he should not allow his murderer to live and, what is even worse, turn his royal bed into a couch for incestuous lust. Whatever he does, however, he should not "taint" his mind by even contemplating anything against his mother but "leave her to heaven" and to her own conscience. As morning is coming, he bids Hamlet a quick farewell with the words, "remember me."

COMMENT: It is interesting that apart from the actual story of the murder and adultery, the ghost did not tell Hamlet anything he did not already suspect and, what is more, the telling was done exactly in terms of Hamlet's own values, as shown in his first soliloquy. There also his father's attributes were held to be far superior to those of Claudius, his mother's lustful change was viewed with disgust, and greater emphasis was placed upon the horror of his mother's infidelity than upon his father's death. This suggests one of two possibilities: either Hamlet takes after his father, as Laertes does after his, or that the ghost is simply telling Hamlet what he wants to hear, justifying his most horrible imaginings so that he may have a reason to take direct action which may damn him. Even the true piece of information he gives him, the manner of the murder, which can be and later is tested, is something that a devil would know and might use to tempt Hamlet to his damnation.

Hamlets' immediate response is to call for help upon all the host of heaven and the earth, and then he has the terrible suspicion that perhaps he had better also call upon the help of hell in remembering his father. But he immediately rejects this suspicion that the ghost may come from hell; "And shall I couple hell? O fie!" Taking hold of himself, he vows to wipe everything from the tablet of his memory except his father's commandment to revenge his murder. But as he thinks of his evil mother and still more of Claudius, a "villain, villain, smiling, damned villain," he suddenly begins to lose control of his reason. He feels he has discovered a wonderful truth that he must write down in the notebook he carries with him to record memorable sayings, and he writes "that one may smile, and smile, and be a villain." Such a statement is, of course, neither a brilliant discovery nor an especially well phrased observation and so would not normally be written down. But that Hamlet is not in a normal frame of mind is immediately shown when he responds to his friends' calling to him with a falconer's cry used for summoning his hawk: "Hillo, ho, ho, boy! Come, bird, come." They ask him for his news and, after pledging them to secrecy, reveals that any "villain dwelling in all Denmark" is a thorough "knave" or scoundrel. To this Horatio well responds: "There needs no ghost, my lord, come from the grave to tell us this." Hamlet agrees and somewhat hysterically says that they should part, the others to their business and he to pray. Horatio notes: "These are but wild and whirling words, my lord," again indicating that Hamlet is not in a rational state.

Hamlet collects himself for a moment and tells them that "it is an honest ghost," that is, the true spirit of his father rather than a devil who has assumed his form, but that he cannot tell them what they said to each other. He now asks them once again to swear that they will never reveal what they have seen tonight, but they feel insulted that Hamlet should ask them again what they have already promised him. Hamlet continues that he wants them now to formally swear to this upon his sword and, as they continue to hesitate, the ghost cries from under the stage, "swear." This once again unsettles Hamlet's reason and he becomes hysterical, saying to the ghost: "Ha, ha, boy, say'st thou so? Art thou there, true-penny." He tells them to swear as they "hear this fellow in the cellarage." They shift ground but the ghost continues to follow them under the stage, repeatedly telling them to "swear by his sword." At this point Hamlet exclaims to the ghost: "Well said, old mole! Canst work i' th' earth so fast? O worthy pioner!"

> **COMMENT:** During his meeting with the ghost, Hamlet was convinced that this was the true spirit of his father. Immediately thereafter, as he is swearing by heaven that he will carry out his father's command, a slight suspicion rises that it may after all have been a devil from hell. He rejects this idea but, as he thinks of his revenge, his mind becomes unsettled, a possibility Horatio had stressed in the event the ghost proved to be an evil spirit. Hamlet gains control of his reason and tells Horatio that the ghost was "honest" rather than a devil, but, as the ghost cries out from the several places beneath the platform, Hamlet's reason again becomes unsettled and he treats him as though he were a familiar devil with whom he had made a pact. Devils were often compared to "pioners" (miners) or "moles" in that they worked underground and were even thought to mine for treasure. Furthermore, Hamlet's complete lack of respect would not be fitting to the true ghost of his father. However much Hamlet's reason may tell him that this is "an honest ghost," then, he has a lurking suspicion that it may, in fact, be a devil and this suspicion acts to unsettle his reason. In addition, the ghost not only acts like a devil in the last part of the scene, but his effect upon Hamlet has been devilish, which continues the audience's own uncertainty as to the true nature of the ghost.

Hamlet once more returns to rationality, but his unsettling experience with the supernatural causes him to tell Horatio: "There are more things in heaven and earth, Horatio, / Than are dreamt of in your philosophy." Though the supernatural appears mysterious to Hamlet, his experience with it causes him to grant it a validity which Horatio's earlier scepticism would have denied. He now tells them that they should be careful not to give any indication, whether by look or word, that they know anything about this night as he may later think it necessary "to put an antic disposition on," that is, to act as though he were insane.

> **COMMENT:** As Hamlet does periodically act insanely for much of the remainder of the play and as he here says that he is going to consciously put on an act of madness for his own purposes, the question has long been argued as to the true nature of Hamlet's madness. Though this question can never be answered with any certainty, the fact that Hamlet's sanity had begun to totter before he got the idea of playing mad is significant. It suggests that Hamlet may have decided to play mad because he is afraid of actually going mad and can use the role of madness to mask and relieve his true psychological instability. It is true that in the original story the Hamlet character assumes the role of madness to further and conceal his investigation of the king, but Shakespeare's Hamlet makes little if any use of his assumed madness in this way, and so the psychological interpretation of Hamlet's assumed madness seems more justified.

Horatio and Marcellus now formally swear to keep Hamlet's two secrets, the meeting with the ghost and Hamlet's assumed madness, and they now prepare to part. Before leaving, however, Hamlet says, "The time is out of joint. O cursed spite / That ever I was born to set it right!"

> **COMMENT:** Hamlet sees his mission of revenge as one of social reform. We have seen this impulse to change the world rather than to accept its evils in his earlier moments of satire, and the ghost has now given this impulse a positive direction and purpose. But, however much part of Hamlet may desire to cause a drastic change in the world, the other part of him desires only to withdraw from this evil world and may provide a constitutional hindrance to the easy accomplishment of his assigned task. When the ghost had first appeared, Hamlet had said: "My fate cries out." But now he considers it spiteful of fate to have assigned him a task so difficult for a person like himself to carry out—how difficult we shall see in the remainder of the play.

SUMMARY These two scenes accomplish the following purposes in closing the first act:

1. Claudius, who impressed us favorably in the second scene, is now revealed to have been the murderer of his brother after having committed adultery with his wife. This places his Christian advice to Hamlet about accepting the evil of the world as the will of heaven in a new light.

2. Hamlet is given the task to revenge his father's murder and rid his court of evil. This task is given supernatural sanction, which may indicate that, as Horatio said, "Heaven will direct it." This is especially possible since Claudius has been shown to be an improper spokesman for the will of heaven. There are, however, strong counter suggestions that the ghost may be a devil and that Hamlet may be endangering his life and soul in following his commands.

3. Two reasons are given which may help to explain Hamlet's later delay in carrying out his assigned task:

   a. The uncertain nature of the ghost, which is the main theme of the first act. Hamlet's own uncertainty, which carries with it an uncertainty as to whether the ghost's commands ought to be followed, has already troubled him to the point of mental instability.

   b. Hamlet's melancholic and generally unstable state of mind, shown in the second scene. The former quality causes Hamlet to feel that he is personally unsuited to the active role of the revenger; the latter, already increased to near insanity by his confusing encounter with the ghost, may make it difficult for him to concentrate rationally upon the act of revenge.

4. The act had begun by showing us first an ominous ghost and then an apparently well ordered state. It ends with Hamlet in the power of the ghost, sworn to overthrow the state, mentally unstable and considering further assuming the role of madness. The action of the play, the course of Hamlet's revenge, has now been determined. The introduction of situation, characters and theme now completed, the stage is set for action.

ACT II: SCENE 1

We are once again in the rooms of Polonius, and Polonius is seen sending off his servant, Reynaldo, to Paris with money and letters for his son, Laertes. He tells Reynaldo that he should inquire about the behavior of Laertes before he visits him. Reynaldo, who seems to know his master's ways very well, tells Polonius that he had already intended to do this and is well praised for this in turn. Polonius now instructs him in some of the refinements of spying. He is to find some Danish acquaintances of Laertes and casually bring up the subject of Laertes. He is then to suggest that Laertes is a libertine, that he gambles, duels, swears and goes to brothels. Reynaldo objects that this would dishonor Laertes, but Polonius explains that this will draw out, either by agreement or denial, the truth about Laertes' behavior as it has been seen by these other Danes. In the middle of this explanation, Polonius forgets what he wants to say and has to be reminded of what he had just said by Reynaldo. Polonius then concludes with a generalization about his tactics, that it is wisdom to be devious in approaching one's target for one can best "by indirections find directions out." Satisfied that Reynaldo has learned his lesson, Polonius bids him goodbye but with a final order to make sure that Laertes is keeping up his musical studies.

COMMENT: In this scene we see the absent-minded old man give Reynaldo the true fruits of his life-long experience, not the high moralizing about integrity he gave to Laertes, but the knowledge of successful spying and falsehood which has become almost second nature to him. His conclusion is doubly significant to the play, for we shall see that all attempts at direct planning are doomed to failure.

Ophelia now enters in a very frightened condition. She explains that, as she was sewing alone in her room, Hamlet had entered in a very disordered state, his jacket unlaced, without a hat, his stockings dirty and hanging down ungartered to his ankles, his knees knocking together, "And with a look so piteous in purport / As if he had been loosèd out of hell / To speak of horrors." He had taken hold of her wrist and held her hard at arm's length with one hand while his other hand was held over his brow. Staying a long time in this position, he observed her face with the intense concentration of one who would draw it. At last, shaking her arm a little and nodding to himself three times in silent agreement with something, he made such a pitiful and deep sigh that it seemed capable of ending his life. He then let her go and went out of the room, but as he left his head was turned over his shoulder and he continued to stare at her until he was out of the door.

COMMENT: When last we saw Hamlet, his mind had been unsettled by his meeting with the ghost, which raised further questions about the nature of this ghost. Ophelia's comment that he now looked "as if he had been loosèd out of hell to speak of horrors" strengthens the view even further that the ghost has been playing a devilish role towards Hamlet both in his disclosures and commands, for Hamlet's soul now appears to be in the power of hell.

As this scene comes right after the scene with the ghost and as nothing has yet been said about any passage of time, its dramatic effect upon the spectator is to reinforce the evidence of the ghost scene. In Act III: Scene 2, Ophelia reveals that two months have passed since the events in Act I. But, as we shall see, when Ophelia says that it is "twice two months" since his father died, Hamlet replies, "die two months ago, and not forgotten yet?" This indicates that, for Hamlet, time has stopped since his encounter with the ghost, for this occurred on the day when, in his first soliloquy, Hamlet had said that his father was "but two months dead, nay, not so much, not two."

In terms of Hamlet's psychology, then, as well as of dramatic effect, the scene with Ophelia seems to be a direct effect of his encounter with the ghost. In despair over the ghost's disclosures about his mother's incestuous adultery with his uncle, Hamlet comes to his beloved's room to search her face for some proof that she is not like his mother. But, as he searches her frightened face he seems to find only confirmation for what he feared, as his nodding head and anguished sigh reveal. Furthermore, he has some justification for his disillusionment with her. As we immediately learn, Ophelia, following her father's orders, has rejected Hamlet's advances after having first been most obliging. Her face may look innocent, as it most assuredly does, but this only proves her falseness, that, like his mother to his father, she can appear loving and then immediately change her behavior. And as he looks so deeply into her eyes, he may perceive some potentiality for lust which nobody should suspect but which is later revealed by the sensual vulgarity she displays in her insanity. Finally, even in this scene she fails him, for she stands with mute terror at the sight of his anguish and does nothing to try to understand or calm him. The effect of this is to destroy whatever lingering love he may still have felt for her and to confirm his belief in the frailty of all women.

Polonius decides that Hamlet is suffering from frustrated love and, forgetful once more, asks Ophelia whether she has quarrelled with him. She replies: "No, my good lord; but as you did command / I did repel his letters and denied / His access to me." Polonius, having forgotten all about his hasty command, now concludes that this is the source of Hamlet's madness. He now makes an unusual admission about his own character; he admits that she showed poor judgement with regards to Hamlet's intentions but excuses this on the grounds of old age: "By heaven, it is as proper to our age / To cast beyond ourselves in our opinions / As it is common for the younger sort / To lack discretion." Old age, he says, is given to authoritarian presumption of its wisdom while having lost the power of true judgement. He now decides to take Ophelia to the King with this discovery as to the source of Hamlet's madness.

SUMMARY This scene accomplishes the following purposes:

1. It confirms our opinion of Polonius from his own mouth, showing him to be a foolish, authoritarian old man who yet prides himself on his power of intrigue. The scene begins with Polonius' instructions to Reynaldo as to how he should spy upon his son and ends with his going to Claudius with, as we shall see, new plans for spying. In both of these instances he shows no more respect or regard for the true feelings of his children than he did for Hamlet's: he is sending his servant to spy upon his son and violating his daughter's modesty and feelings by bringing her before the King in order to advance his own position in the King's respect, to prove to him that, despite his advancing age, he is just as good a counselor-of-state as he ever was under the late King Hamlet.

2. The narrated scene in Ophelia's room (called "closet" in Elizabethan times) serves three purposes:

   a. It continues the thematic questioning of the ghost's true identity, reinforcing the suspicion that it is actually a devil, since Hamlet's soul has been reduced to a state of hell.

   b. It introduces through narration the change in Hamlet's behavior and attire before we actually see him. In Act I: Scene 2, we were told that Hamlet was dressed in complete mourning but there was nothing said of any disarray. Now we are told that his clothing is completely disordered and dirty. John Dover Wilson suggests that this is the way he is to dress for much of the remainder of the play: it is the sign of his assumed madness, though his emotional disturbance over Ophelia seems genuine enough.

   c. It shows that Hamlet's continuing disturbance over the infidelity of his mother has now affected his ability to love Ophelia, and it marks his last moment of genuine involvement with her while she lives.

ACT II: SCENE 2

The scene shifts to a room in the castle where Claudius and Gertrude are greeting Rosencrantz and Guildenstern. These gentlemen are boyhood friends of Hamlet whom Claudius has recalled to Denmark in the hope that they may be able to help him investigate the nature of Hamlet's increasing mental disorder. His "transformation," earlier described by Ophelia, seems to Claudius to have resulted from more than simply his father's death, and he hopes that by discovering the reason for this these friends may help him to restore Hamlet's health. The Queen seconds this with the promise of an ample reward, and they agree to help the King.

> **COMMENT:** This scene indicates that there has been some passage of time during which Hamlet's behavior has become increasingly mad. Whether Hamlet has achieved anything by this means we do not yet know, but we do know that it has caused speculation in the court and sufficient worry on Claudius' part for him to have sent for two spies to investigate Hamlet. Whereas earlier he was anxious only to gain Hamlet's goodwill, Hamlet's "madness" has now placed Claudius on his guard against him. Polonius' delight to have discovered, as he thinks, the cause of Hamlet's "madness" and his immediate going to Claudius with the news show how concerned the court and particularly Claudius had become with the topic of Hamlet's "madness."

Polonius enters with the news of the return of the ambassadors to Norway. He then says: "And I do think—or else this brain of mine / Hunts not the trail of policy so sure / As it hath used to do —that I have found / The very cause of Hamlet's lunacy." (If Polonius was forced in the last scene to admit that his lack of judgment was a symptom of old age, he now hopes to dispel any similar doubt that Claudius may have about his continuing usefulness.) Claudius is more anxious to hear of this than of the results of his ambassadors: "O, speak of that! That do I long to hear." But Polonius asks that the ambassadors be attended to first and Claudius agrees. While Polonius goes to bring in the ambassadors, Claudius tells his "dear Gertrude" that Polonius thinks he has discovered the source of her son's disorder, but she is convinced that she already knows the reason: "I doubt it is no other but the main / His father's death and our o'er-hasty marriage."

> **COMMENT:** This private conference reveals two things about Gertrude: good insight into her son's character (as these were the original reasons for Hamlet's despair), and lack of any possible knowledge of her former husband's murder. It is interesting that while Claudius had only mentioned his father's death as a possible reason for Hamlet's madness, Gertrude is also sensitive to the effect her hasty remarriage has had upon her son. Claudius' term of endear-

ment towards her also indicates that his feelings for her far exceed lust, as will be shown more fully later on.

Voltemand now enters with the news of his successful mission to Norway; the King of Norway, upon investigating Fortinbras' activities, had found Claudius to be correct and, very grieved by this, had restrained his nephew from attacking Denmark. He has, however, decided to deploy Fortinbras and the force he has raised against Poland, and now asks Claudius' permission for the safe passage of these troops through Denmark on their way to Poland. Claudius' immediate reaction to this is positive but he is far too impatient to hear Polonius' theory about Hamlet to give his full attention to this matter now. Telling the ambassadors that they will feast together at night, he bids them retire now and turns to Polonius.

Although saying that "brevity is the soul of wit," Polonius is so long-winded about getting to the point that the Queen finally interrupts him with the words, "more matter, with less art." But Polonius continues awhile with comically pretentious rhetoric until he finally gets to the point: his daughter has obediently given him a love letter to her from Hamlet. He now proceeds to read this letter which almost rivals his own comic speeches in its over-wrought, conventional love melancholy. Claudius, satisfied with Hamlet's love for Ophelia, asks Polonius how she has received his love, and he replies his duty towards the King led him to tell his daughter that, as the Prince was so far above her, "she should lock herself from his resort, / Admit no messengers, receive no tokens." She had done this and the result of this rejection of his love, Polonius concludes, has led to Hamlet's progressive madness. Claudius asks Gertrude whether she thinks this is the reason, and she replies, "It may be, very like." Polonius claims that his advice has always been correct and that they should behead him "if this be otherwise."

Claudius now asks him what they might do to further investigate his theory and Polonius suggests a plan with which he had evidently come prepared. He says that there is a spot near where they are standing where Hamlet often walks for four hours at a time. "At such a time I'll loose my daughter to him," he suggests, while the King and he will observe from behind a hanging tapestry the nature of their encounter. If this does not prove his case, he concludes, "Let me be no assistant for a state / But keep a farm and carters." The King agrees to try Polonius' plan, whereupon Hamlet enters.

COMMENT: John Dover Wilson in *What Happens in Hamlet* has proposed the theory, which has recently gained widespread critical and theatrical acceptance, that Hamlet entered unobserved at the back of the stage before his announced entrance and thus overheard the plot. Such a theory seriously alters the usual reading of this later scene, as shall be discussed at that time. Although Mr. Wilson argues his case very persuasively, it is by no means proven. A second point about this last portion of the scene is the complete reduction of Polonius to a comic figure, posturing ridiculously about both his verbal style and his subtle reasoning, though we may note a touch of increasing insecurity about his value to the state.

The Queen notes how "sadly the poor wretch comes reading," and Polonius begs them to leave him alone with Hamlet. He tries to make conversation with Hamlet but Hamlet counters everything he says with apparently mad but actually quite satiric thrusts. He calls Polonius a "fishmonger," which also meant a pimp, and tells him that he had better not let his daughter walk in the sun as she may conceive spontaneously like maggots.

COMMENT: Wilson uses this to support his theory that Hamlet overheard Polonius' conference with the King, since Polonius' statement to "loose" his daughter to him is language which an Elizabethan procurer would use in reference to his whore. In any case, Hamlet is speaking very coarsely about Ophelia.

Polonius, further convinced by this that Hamlet's madness has resulted from his disappointed love, now asks him what he is reading. After bandying about with this for a while, Hamlet finally says that he is reading slanders against old age by a "satirical rogue" who says that "old men have grey beards, that their faces are wrinkled" and "that they have a plentiful lack of wit, together with most weak hams," all of which, though he agrees with it, he does not think it decent to write down since Polonius, himself, is old. At this Polonius silently comments, "Though this be madness, yet there is method in't." After a few more lines in which Hamlet shows a disconcerting wit, Polonius decides to leave and says, "I will most humbly take my leave of you." Hamlet begins to return this satirically but then his mood abruptly changes: "You cannot, sir, take from me anything that I will more willingly part withal— except my life, except my life, except my life." After Polonius starts to leave, Hamlet expresses his final disgust with Polonius: "These tedious old fools!"

COMMENT: This is the first glimpse we gain of Hamlet's supposed "madness" and we see it take the form of brilliant but savage satirical wit. Hamlet is using the post of madness here as a license to say anything he feels like saying. That he genuinely feels Polonius to be a tedious old fool and has no use for such people we know from his own statement, but his role of madman permits him to make unmerciful fun of Polonius. Indeed, Hamlet here exhibits an extreme hatred and bitterness towards Polonius. This might be explained by Hamlet's awareness of Polonius' interference with his love and, possibly, Polonius' plan to use Ophelia against him in the service of his enemy, Claudius. Our respect for Polonius has been so reduced by this time, however, that we can hardly blame Hamlet for his treatment of him. In his last lines to Polonius, moreover, we see that Hamlet is still in the same psychological state in which we first saw him, the rapid alternation between destructive satire and self-destructive melancholy, between hysteria and depression.

Rosencrantz and Guildenstern now enter and are happily greeted by Hamlet as "My excellent good friends!" After some introductory kidding with them about the state of their fortune, he asks them what they have done to deserve being sent here to "prison." When they question Hamlet's reference to Denmark as a prison, he replies: "Why, then 'tis none to you, for there is nothing either good or bad but thinking makes it so. To me it is a prison." Seizing this opportunity to begin their investigation, they suggest, "Why, then your ambition makes it one." After arguing this point, he asks them again, in the "way of friendship," what they are doing at Elsinore. They reply that they have come simply to visit him. Hamlet thanks them for this but then immediately asks whether it is a free visit or whether they were sent for by the King and Queen. They hesitate to answer him; he asks them again; and, as they finally confer on an answer, Hamlet says to himself, "Nay then, I have an eye of you." They finally do admit, "My lord, we were sent for," but it is too late—Hamlet's trust has been alienated. In one of the most beautiful speeches in the play, Hamlet now explains to them why they were sent for: "I have of late—but wherefore I know not—lost all my mirth." In his depressed state the good earth seems to him "a sterile promontory," the majestic heavens appear "nothing to him but a foul and pestilent congregation of vapors," man, himself, with his noble reason, infinite faculties and beauty, seems to him the "quintessence of dust."

COMMENT: Hamlet here explains the source of his statement that "there is nothing either good or bad but thinking makes it so," that our understanding of objective reality depends upon our perception of it which differs from individual to individual and from time to time. Although Hamlet's reason and memory tell him that the earth, heavens and man are beautiful and meaningful, something in his spirit has made him no longer able to perceive them that way. Life and the heavens seem sterile and meaningless because man can only come to dust. Why it is he should feel this so deeply that it has warped his whole perception of existence, however, he admits that he does not know. Although he is countering their earlier suggestion, which evidently came from Claudius, that it is disappointed ambition, there is also about his words the tone of true confession. Hamlet is to continue through most of the play to try to analyze what it is that has placed him in this psychological state of depressed inactivity and general irrationality; Claudius and his followers also try to analyze Hamlet's condition, as we have seen; finally, all critics of the play for three hundred years have tried to explain this central mystery at the heart of the play. Hamlet's statement here, then, is the starting point for the "problem of Hamlet."

Rosencrantz and Guildenstern now tell Hamlet of the coming of a company of actors and there is some discussion between them of acting companies which reflects the conditions in the Elizabethan theatre at the time, Before the players enter, however, Hamlet tells Rosencrantz and Guildenstern that they are welcome to Elsinore. More than this, he also tells them that Claudius and Gertrude are deceived about his madness, that he is only mad when he feels like it and can otherwise be perfectly sane, as indeed has been shown in this scene with them.

COMMENT: Since Hamlet has already concluded that they are spies, he is very careless in making this important admission to them. This can only be explained as forgetfulness on Hamlet's part due to his enjoyment of their company, to his ability to discuss with them such varied topics as the state of his soul and the condition of theatrical companies. This is one of the first signs of Hamlet's lack of precaution in his dealings with Claudius, as opposed to Claudius' many precautions throughout the play.

Polonius now enters with the players. He introduces them with comical pretentiousness which leads Hamlet once again to make fun of him in the role of madman. Hamlet now welcomes the players and asks them as a proof of their quality to recite a speech from one of their plays about the death of Priam, the old King of Troy, which he begins. Hamlet's delivery is praised by Polonius and then the player continues: Pyrrhus drives at Priam but "in rage strikes wide." Nonetheless, Priam, the "unnerved father," falls from the wind of Pyrrhus' sword. Instead of killing him then, however, "his sword, / Which was declining on the milky head / Of reverend Priam, seemed i' the' air to stick" and, against his own will, "did nothing." Finally however, "aroused vengeance sets him new awork" and never did blows fall like those now on Priam. He now continues with an impassioned speech on Hecuba's grief over the death of her husband, Priam. Hamlet is delighted with the player's recitation and asks him whether the company could play "The Murder of Gonzago" that night with an insertion of a speech of "some dozen or sixteen lines" which he would write himself. The player agrees to do this and Hamlet tells Polonius to see that they are well looked after, upon which they all depart, leaving Hamlet alone.

COMMENT: The speech that Hamlet remembers and wants to hear recited is interesting as a reflection of Hamlet's own preoccupations. In the speech a revenger is at first unable to commit revenge, but can only act wildly. This, however, disarms his opponent and eventually he is able to accomplish his revenge with great vigor. The situation parallels Hamlet's own plight. Months have passed and instead of sweeping to his revenge as he had told the ghost he would do, he has only acted madly. That he is beginning to feel some guilt about this delay is shown by his remembrance of this speech with its similar mad delay in revenge. He hopes to quiet his conscience by remembering that a similar revenger finally did accomplish his purposes. But the guilt only further emerges when he is alone.

We now come to Hamlet's second soliloquy. Hamlet begins with the exclamation: "O, what a rogue and peasant slave am I!" It seems monstrous to him that the player could so work himself up "for nothing, / For Hecuba! / What's Hecuba to him, or he to Hecuba, / That he should weep for her?" He wonders "what would he do / Had he the motive and the cue for passion / That I have?" Though the player, with such real motivation would "make mad the guilty," he, "a dull and muddy-mettled rascal," moans about in a dream without any real feeling for his cause and "can say nothing," no, not even for a dear King who was cursedly murdered. He then asks himself whether he is a "coward." At first he is horrified by such a humiliating suggestion, but then he concedes that it must be so, that "I am pigeon-livered and lack gall / To make oppression bitter" since he has not yet fattened the vultures with Claudius' guts. He then tries to work up a passion against Claudius by yelling: "Bloody, bawdy villain! Remorseless, treacherous, lecherous, kindless villain! / O, vengeance!" But then he immediately realizes, "Why, what an ass am I!" This is some bravery, that the son of a dear murdered father, "prompted to my revenge by heaven and hell," must release the feelings of his heart simply with words rather than with action.

He now finally puts his brains to work upon the revenge. He remembers having heard "that guilty creatures sitting at a play" which represented their own crime have been so struck by guilt that they have confessed their crime. He decides (apparently having already forgotten that he had just instructed the players to do the same thing) that he will "have these players / Play something like the murther of my father / Before mine uncle. I'll observe his looks" and if he but flinches "I know my course." This is the first time we have seen Hamlet express any doubt about his course, but the reason he gives is one that he may well have entertained:

> The spirit that I have seen
> May be a devil, and the devil hath power
> T' assume a pleasing shape, yea, and perhaps
> Out of my weakness and my melancholy,
> As he is very potent with such spirits,
> Abuses me to damn me.

He decides that he needs further objective proof of Claudius' guilt and that "The play's the thing / Wherein I'll catch the conscience of the king."

COMMENT: The second soliloquy shows us the following important things about about Hamlet:

1.　Hamlet has not been able to concentrate on the subject of his revenge for reasons that he cannot understand. When a chance circumstance does cause him to think about it, he feels guilt which, in turn, causes him to rationalize about his delay. Not that his suspicion about the ghost is not valid, but it is an after-thought to explain his delay rather than its actual cause.

2.　We see, however, that when Hamlet does think about his revenge he is caught up in a conflict of values. This conflict, which has persisted throughout Western culture and was particularly strong during the Renaissance, is that between the honor code and the religious code. The honor code was the mark which distinguished the aristocrat from the "peasant slave." His "gall" was quickly raised by any sign of "oppression" or humiliation and he was always ready to bravely risk his life to vindicate his honor or the honor of his family. One of the obligations of a man of honor was to revenge the death of his father; not to do this was to be a "coward," the mark of the "peasant slave" who desired only to preserve his life whatever the cost. When, however, dishonor was

inevitable, the honor code preached suicide as the only
way of proving one's superiority to his fate. The man of
honor aspired to greatness and was only afraid of shame.
In contrast to this, the religious code preached that goodness was superior to greatness. The signs of the "great
soul" according to the honor code, its willingness to
commit murderous revenge or suicide were mortal sins
according to religious interpretation. Goodness expresses
itself not through a vaunting superiority to fate but a
humble acceptance of whatever heaven may send. As
Job says in the Bible, "The Lord giveth and the Lord
taketh away. Blessed be the name of the Lord." As a
Christian gentleman, Hamlet is pulled by both of these
opposing codes of values. He cannot bear the thought
of dishonor, though the vindication of his honor and
nobility can only be accomplished through murder, and
he is also anxious to secure the salvation of his soul
which premeditated murder would place in danger of
damnation. The "Christian gentleman" was a contradic-
tion in terms since such a character desired to avoid both
shame in this world and damnation in the next and he
could not have it both ways.

3. If this conflict in values is not the primary cause of
Hamlet's delay and mental disorder, which remains mysterious, it is of primary thematic importance for the
play, for it is by means of these codes that we are asked
to evaluate Hamlet. Thus it is the spectator as well as
Hamlet who must decide which of these codes is to be
preferred, and it is also in terms of this question that
the ghost is to be judged. If the ghost is demanding of
Hamlet that which will damn him, and if the question
of salvation is more important than that of honor, then
the spectator should seriously entertain with Hamlet the
possibility that the ghost may be a devil who has been
attracted by his melancholy to tempt him into a damnable
murder. It may well be, then, that Hamlet is ethically
right to delay his revenge even though the question of
ethics is not the primary source of the delay.

SUMMARY   This scene accomplishes the following purposes:

1. It exhibits Hamlet's assumed madness in both words and behavior and starts the theorizing as to its source: Polonius
believes it comes from disappointed love; Rosencrantz and
Guildenstern, probably from a cue by Claudius, believe it
results from frustrated ambition for the throne; Gertrude
believes it results simply from Hamlet's shock at the death of

his father and her hasty remarriage; and Hamlet is at a loss to explain the drastic inner change that has come over him.

2. It begins the cross plotting of the chief characters against each other. Hamlet's assumed madness, decided upon at the end of Act I, which was supposed to achieve some unspecified and probably unthought of purpose, has now so raised Claudius' suspicions that he has sent to Rosencrantz and Guildenstern to spy upon Hamlet, which they begin to do in this scene. Polonius plans to test his theory by confronting Hamlet with his daughter while Claudius and he spy upon the meeting from behind a tapestry. Hamlet plans to test the ghost's truth and Claudius' guilt through the performance of a play upon a similar crime which he will revise for this purpose. These last two plots are to occupy much of the first two scenes of Act III.

3. It further exhibits the character of Hamlet, his savage wit towards Polonius (who has become little more than a pretentious fool), his profound reflective quality in conversation with Rosencrantz and Guildenstern, his delight to see them and also the players, his love of the theatre, and his savage attack upon himself, combined with his lack of personal understanding.

ACT III: SCENE 1

The scene is set in the room in the castle where the planned encounter of Hamlet and Ophelia is to take place. The King and Queen are present surrounded by Polonius, Ophelia, Rosencrantz, Guildenstern and other lords. Claudius is in the midst of asking Rosencrantz and Guildenstern whether they have discovered anything concerning the cause of Hamlet's madness, but they answer that Hamlet "with a crafty madness" has kept from "confession of his true state." Gertrude asks them how he received them and whether they have been able to interest him in any pastime. They reply that he treated them like a gentleman and was overjoyed by their news of the arrival of a company of players whom he has already ordered to appear this night before him. Polonius says that Hamlet has also asked the King and Queen to attend the performance, and Claudius says that he is happy to hear of Hamlet's new interest and to support it by attendance.

Rosencrantz and Guildenstern now leave and Claudius suggests that Gertrude leave also as he has secretly sent for Hamlet that he may accidentally meet Ophelia. Claudius and Polonius mean to spy on the encounter to test whether Polonius' theory of the source of

Hamlet's madness, disappointed love, is correct. Gertrude tells Ophelia that she hopes Ophelia is "the happy cause of Hamlet's madness" and that, if her virtues are able to cure him, there would be a hope for their marriage. As Ophelia seconds her hope, Gertrude leaves. Polonius now instructs Opelia that, while the King and he hide themselves, she is to walk there by herself reading a pious book since this would serve to explain her lonely presence. He now reflects, as well he might, that people are often to blame for covering evil behavior with a show of "pious action." In an "aside" (a speech spoken to the audience and meant to indicate silent thought), Claudius reveals that Polonius' words have stung his conscience, for he too covers his deed with behavior as false as a harlot's painted charms. The maintenance of this falsehood has become so difficult for him that he must cry out, "O heavy burden!"

COMMENT: This is the first objective proof we have had to substantiate the ghost's charges against Claudius, for he admits an unspecified evil "deed." In this admission, furthermore, we see that Claudius does have an essentially moral nature, for his conscience can become anguished by a chance remark. This also prepares us for Claudius' hysterical breakdown during the performance of the play in the next scene. All of this shows us that Claudius is not naturally evil and is oppressed both by the guilt of having committed evil and by the falseness he has to assume to cover the fact of his guilt.

As Hamlet is now heard approaching, Claudius and Polonius withdraw behind the painted tapestry to watch his encounter with Ophelia.

Hamlet enters so involved with his own thoughts that he does not at first see Ophelia. We now hear the famous "To be or not to be" soliloquy. He begins by questioning which is the "nobler" code of behavior, that which bids one "to be," to live even though this means "to suffer" from "outrageous fortune," or that which bids one "not to be," to commit suicide and thus "end" one's suffering through the act of "opposing" the outrage which fortune would do him. "To die," he reasons, is "to sleep—no more," and by such a sleep it is possible to "end the heartache, and the thousand natural shocks" that human beings inherit in the process of being born. Such an end to human troubles, he concludes is "a consummation devoutly to be wished." "To die," he repeats, is "to sleep," but in sleep, he now remembers, there is also the possibility of dreams and this creates a new difficulty. For when we have cast off the difficulties of life "in that sleep of death," we do not know "what dreams may come," and this must cause us to hesitate before commiting suicide. This is what causes people to endure the "calamity" of a "long life." For who would bear the injuries of existence, the wrongs and humiliations of oppression, "the pangs of despised love," the delay in both law and position which those with merit must patiently bear from the unworthy and insolent people who do receive high office, who would bear the general burdens of "a weary life,

> But that the dread of something after death,
> The undiscovered country, from whose bourn
> [confinement]
> No traveller returns, puzzles the will,
> And makes us rather bear those ills we have
> Than fly to others that we know not of?

This consciousness of the religious problem involved with suicide, the dread of eternal punishment, "does make cowards of us all," and "the pale cast of thought" sickens the power of "resolution," and this not only with regards to suicide but to all great "enterprises," whose force is similarly turned away into inaction through overconsideration. He now sees Ophelia at her prayers and tells her to include in them "all my sins."

COMMENT: In our last view of Hamlet during the "rogue and peasant slave" soliloquy, we saw Hamlet in a state of guilt over his long inaction which was resolved by a new commitment to a course of positive action. Now, but a few hours later, we see him sunk once more in suicidal melancholy, forgetful of the whole question of his revenge. He is, however, still concerned by the conflict between the honor and religious codes, but it is now centered on the question of suicide rather than murder. As either course, however, would lead him into mortal sin, he does well to tell Ophelia to pray for "all my sins." Though prompted by honor first to revenge and now to suicide, his religious beliefs inhibit him from taking such action.

But the power of his religion over him is more negative than positive; it is fear of eternal punishment rather than the value of righteousness which motivates him. As fear, however, is an ignoble emotion, his sense of honor arises once more to accuse him of cowardice, just as it did in the previous soliloquy. He concludes that the reason for the cowardly inaction which he despises in himself is that he thinks too much and overintellectualizes his problems to the point of inertia. Hamlet's conclusion here has been accepted by the great nineteenth century English poet and critic, Samuel Taylor Coleridge, as the solution to the problem of Hamlet's inactivity, and it has remained one of the standard critical approaches to the play although it is less in favor at present. To return to our earlier discussion, we see that as long as the power of Hamlet's religion over him is a negative one, it cannot destroy the influence of the honor code upon his spirit, but simply inhibits its power to motivate sustained positive action. The result is that Hamlet remains a prey to the worst effects of both codes, guilt and shame, which has the additional result of driving him still further into suicidal melancholy. He has but to think of taking action, as he does in the second soliloquy, and he becomes so overwhelmed by internal conflicts, that he soon can desire nothing but suicide, as we see in the third soliloquy. But this in turn produces its own vicious cycle of guilt, followed by shame which proceeds to such a point that he feels shackled by his very consciousness of such thoughts, and blames them in turn for his inactivity.

It is, however, the nature of his conflicts, part of which he admits that he does not himself understand, which produces his inertia rather than any overintellectualizing he may do about them. The inertia is there; the intellectualizing comes afterwards as an attempt to understand the inactivity and then becomes useful to Hamlet as a means of rationalizing his unfathomed apathy and melancholy. As we have seen in the two past soliloquies, Hamlet thinks about his problems just to the point at which he can develop some rationalization for his inactivity, (in the second soliloquy it is doubt about the ghost's nature, in the third soliloquy it is overintellectualization of his problems), and then he concludes his inner investigations, fully satisfied for the time.

One other interesting statement he makes here is that "no traveller returns" from "the undiscovered country" of death. Such a statement would deny that the ghost was the spirit of his father returned from death and would indicate that the doubt about the ghost had grown stronger in the interval between the two soliloquies. This in turn would free him from the sense of obligation to commit revenge, and so the necessity for life, and enable him more freely to contemplate suicide. But this statement also indicates a weakening of his religious convictions to a point of agnosticism, further showing the negative quality of his religion and perhaps even a result of the ever more deadening effect of religious commandments upon his impulses. This agnosticism, however, is important for tragedy which requires the spectator to feel that death is dreadful. If there were no question that Hamlet was going to heaven at the end of the play (as Horatio claims), his death would not really be tragic.

One final question concerns the form of this soliloquy. There are some modern critics who see it only as an exercise in rhetoric such as Hamlet might have studied at the University of Wittenberg. While it is true that the question form of the soliloquy, with the balancing of two alternatives, is similar to rhetorical exercises of the time and might indicate that Hamlet was using his logical training to attack his personal problems, to dismiss the whole soliloquy as an intellectual exercise or game is going too far, for the first soliloquy is also personally concerned with suicide and Hamlet is immediately to make some further suicidal statements in his scene with Ophelia.

The meeting between Hamlet and Ophelia begins politely as Ophelia asks Hamlet how he has been feeling these past days and he replies that he has been feeling well. She then tells him that she has with her some things he had given her which she has long desired to return to him and prays him now to receive them. He denies having given her anything and she, apparently hurt by this, says that she knows very well that he did and with his presents added such sweet words "as made the things more rich." Since this sweetness is now gone, she bids him take back his presents, for "rich gifts wax poor when givers prove unkind." He then laughs out hysterically and asks her whether she is "honest," and again whether she is "fair" (that is, "white" as is the color of purity and virtue). She does not understand what he is driving at and asks him what he means, to which he answers, "That if you be honest and fair, your honesty should admit no discourse to your beauty," that is, if she were truly virtuous, she would not admit anyone to approach her beauty. She takes his verbal quibble in another sense and asks him whether beauty could do better than to go with honesty. He becomes ever more hysterical and says that she is right, for beauty has such power that it can "transform honesty from what it is to a bawd." Though this seems a paradox, it has recently been proven. He then abruptly claims, "I did love you once." She, still hurt though now apparently vindicated, answers, "Indeed, my lord, you made me believe so." To this Hamlet lashes out at her that she should not have believed him since his stock is so sullied that it is incapable of virtue. He now as abruptly claims, "I loved you not," and she even more sadly replies, "I was the more sadly deceived." He then cries out to her in a long, bitter speech: "Get thee to a nunnery. Why wouldest thou be a breeder of sinners? I am myself indifferent honest, but yet I could accuse me of such things that it were better my mother had not borne

me: I am very proud, revengeful, ambitious, with more offenses
at my beck than I have thoughts to put them in, imagination to
give them shape, or time to act them in. What should such fellows
as I do crawling between earth and heaven? We are arrant knaves
all; believe none of us. Go thy ways to a nunnery." He then
abruptly asks her where her father is and, when she replies that he
is at home, he says that Polonius should be locked in there "that
he may play the fool nowhere but in's own house." He bids her
"farewell," but, as she prays to heaven to help him, he continues that
if she should marry she can take this curse with her that however
chastely she may behave she will still gain a bad reputation. He
tells her again to go to a nunnery, says farewell again, and then
continues that if she must marry she should marry a fool, "for
wise men know well enough what monsters you make of them." He
sends her to a nunnery again, says farewell again, and, as she
prays again to heaven to restore his sanity, he continues his outburst against her, this time directed against women's cosmetics,
"paintings." He charges, "God hath given you one face, and you
make yourselves another." As he continues against the seductive
movements, tones and nicknaming habits of women, he finally
cries out, "Go to, I'll no more on't; it hath made me mad." He
demands that there be no more marriages, though, "all but one" of
those who are married "shall live." He tells her to go to a nunnery
a final time and leaves without another word. Ophelia is left in a
state of shocked despair at the behavior of her former lover. In
a return to poetry after the prose of the last section, she exclaims,
"O, what a noble mind is here o'erthrown!" He who was the ideal
courtier, soldier and scholar, the hope of the state, the model of
fashion and manners, and of a most noble intelligence, is now
completely disordered by madness, while she who received the
sweetness of his love is the most wretched of ladies.

COMMENT: This scene calls for much discussion. The
first point is Ophelia's attitude towards Hamlet and his reaction to this. We see that curiously enough Ophelia acts as
though she were the injured party though we know it was
she who first rejected Hamlet. His amazed question as to
whether she is being honest or hypocritical is, then, natural
enough. Though her sense of injury may have come from
their last, silent meeting (which she recounted to her father)
in which he did, indeed, reject her, she seems to have little
understanding then as now of her own responsibility for his
present behavior towards her. Hamlet's suspicions towards
her may have been aroused not only by her assumption of
innonence but also by her presence, fully prepared with all
the things he had given her, at a place to which he was sum-
moned. His belief that she is playing a hypocritical part with
him may be even further explained by the theory that he

overheard the plan for this meeting and is now remembering this. In any case, he begins to play a part of his own with her, assuming once more his role of madman. But the savagery of his attack on her and the nature of his disclosures about himself indicate that it may not be all an act, that his mind has been truly unsettled behind its assumed madness by this new "proof" of the falseness of a woman he once loved.

This proof further supports the generalization he had made about his mother, "frailty, thy name is woman," and in his continuing attacks he identifies Ophelia more and more with his mother. As he thinks about his mother's lustful nature, however, he begins to doubt his own feelings, since he is her son and has inherited a debased nature from her which may be incapable of any higher feeling than lust. But if his own feelings for Ophelia could not be trusted, neither can any other man's and it were better for Ophelia to leave the world of dishonest men and get to a nunnery. And not only should she not continue the process of breeding sinners, but neither should anyone else; there should be no more marriages, no more sex. (Some critics, following John Dover Wilson, argue that since the term "nunnery" was used in Elizabethan slang to refer to brothels, Hamlet is actually suggesting the opposite of what he appears to be saying, namely, that since she is playing the false part of the harlot with him she may as well drop any pretense of virtue and become a professional whore. This view is further strengthened by Wilson's theory that Hamlet overheard Polonius' slang references to his daughter as a whore, now recognizes that she is being used by her father and is directing this to Polonius' ears as well.)

We have already touched on the second important item, Hamlet's attitude towards himself. We remember that just before the start of this scene, upon seeing "the fair Ophelia," he had asked her to remember his sins in her prayers. Now he says that he could accuse himself "of such things that it were better my mother had not borne me," not only the things which are present to his conscious mind but offenses which he cannot even put into thought, which defy the power of his imagination though he senses them so deeply and is so revolted by them that he cannot see why such a person as he should be allowed even to crawl upon the earth. He feels, however, that it is something for which his mother is ultimately responsible. As he thinks about the whore-like falseness of his mother and Ophelia and all women, with their "paintings" and seductive ways, he cries out for an end to sex, for "it hath made me mad."

Now what all of this means at the very least is a definite sexual nausea: his mother's sensuality has revolted him and the thought that he may have inherited her nature and may be capable of equally base sexual desires is more than he can bear. The famous psychoanalyst, Ernest Jones, who was a student and the biographer of Freud, has suggested a psychoanalytic explanation of these lines and, following Freud, of the whole "problem of Hamlet," namely that Hamlet had an "Oedipus Complex." Freudian theory states that all men at a certain stage of their development subconsciously desire to reenact the crimes of the mythical Greek King, Oedipus, who murdered his father and married his mother. Like all growing children, Hamlet had repressed these forbidden desires and grown up into a model young man. When, however, Hamlet learns that Claudius has murdered Hamlet's father and married his mother, has fulfilled his own repressed desires, his old "Oedipus Complex" is reactivated though still repressed, because it is too horrible to be accepted by his conscious mind. Therefore, he feels suicidally revolted with himself for reasons that he cannot fathom. Moreover, he is subconsciously unable to condemn Claudius for having committed the very crimes he himself desired subconsciously to commit. But since he is not consciously aware of his "Oedipus Complex," he is at a loss to understand the source of his inability to act or even to think in any sustained fashion of such action.

While this theory explains very neatly aspects of the play which are difficult to explain otherwise, particularly Hamlet's obsessed preoccupation with his mother's sexual life, the difficulty with it is that it could not have been Shakespeare's expressed intention since he could not have known of Freud's theories. Jones gets around this difficulty by suggesting that Shakespeare's knowledge of the nature of the "Oedipus Complex" was intuitive since it was also true of himself and since it is generally agreed that Hamlet was Shakespeare's most autobiographical creation. However this may be, Shakespeare could not have been consciously aware of this explanation for Hamlet's behavior, no matter how well he portrayed its symptoms, and this behavior remained for him as for his character, Hamlet, an ultimate mystery.

A final explanation of this scene is based on the theory that Hamlet overheard the plot to test him with Ophelia and that he is here acting a mad role primarily for the benefit of Claudius and Polonius. What is more, he is playing a rather reckless game with them in telling Claudius that he is

"revengeful" and "ambitious." Thus he justifies Claudius'
theory while at the same time warning him that "all but one
shall live," and justifies Polonius' theory that it is women's
false love which "hath made me mad," while at the same
time attacking him directly as a fool and father of a whore.

Finally, Ophelia's closing description of Hamlet, it is generally
agreed, is meant to be viewed as an objective portrait of Hamlet as he was before the death of his father and remarriage
of his mother, which had already affected his state of mind
at the beginnng of the play.

Claudius and Polonius now come out from thier hiding place each
convinced of the truth of his own theory as to Hamlet's condition.
Claudius begins by rejecting outright Polonius' theory about love.
He also notes that "what he spake, though it lacked form a little,
was not like madness." He believes that there is something in
Hamlet's soul which is causing him to brood and which will finally
"hatch" into some "danger." To prevent this eventuality, Claudius
immediately decides to send Hamlet "with speed to England" with
the covering excuse that he going to demand of England the tribute
it owes to Denmark. He tells Polonius that he hopes the change of
surroundings "shall expel this something-settled matter in his heart,"
and asks Polonius what he thinks of the plan. Polonius agrees to
it though he still believes "the origin and commencement of his
grief / Sprung from neglected love." He asks Ophelia how she is
but immediately turns from her to continue his discussion with
Claudius despite his daughter's grief. He now suggests a new spying
plan to Claudius, that after the play Gertrude should send for
Hamlet and ask him to come alone to her room. She should then
ask Hamlet plainly to explain to her what is troubling him. Polonius
will himself be hidden in the room to overhear their conference.
If Gertrude does not discover the source of his melancholy, then
Claudius should send Hamlet to England. Claudius agrees with
Polonius' new plan, concluding "Madness in great ones must not
unwatched go." They leave and the scene ends.

SUMMARY   This scene again contrasts the characters of Claudius and Hamlet as follows:

1. Claudius actively investigates Hamlet's disturbing behavior, first
    with Rosencrantz and Guildenstern and then with Ophelia.
    Though he discovers nothing definite, Hamlet's behavior with
    Ophelia is so threatening to him that he acts with immediate
    decision to send Hamlet to England and thus protect himself.
    Claudius is a man of practical action who does what is neces-
    sary to achieve his goals, whether these be the gaining of a

throne through murder or simple self-preservation. But though Claudius will murder to gain a selfish end, he is not thoroughly evil but feels genuine remorse for what he has done. What he desires most of all is for things to remain as they were at the beginning of the play so that he will not be forced to commit further evil to preserve himself.

2. Hamlet, on the other hand, is still incapable of action. Though he had recently decided on a plan of attack, when we see him now he has returned to suicidal melancholy and to the unsuccessful attempt to explain his behavior and nature. His scene with Ophelia brings out the worst aspect of his character, the almost inhuman savagery he shows to anyone he feels has injured him, here the innocent and too obedient Ophelia. His savagery, however, is verbal, and no matter how he may threaten Claudius, its effect is to place him at a greater disadvantage with regard to its object.

ACT III: SCENE 2

Hamlet enters a hall of the castle explaining to the players how they are to perform. They are to pronounce the words easily rather than mouth them broadly; they are not to "saw the air too much" with their hands "but use all gently"; their passion should be controlled and smooth, for it is offensive to hear a "fellow tear a passion to tatters, to very rags, to split the ears of the groundlings, who for the most part are capable of nothing but inexplicable dumb shows and noise." But neither should they be too tame. He tells them to "suit the action to the word, the word to the action, with this special observance, that you o'erstep not the modesty of nature," for the purpose of drama from its origin to the present "was and is, to hold, as 'twere, the mirror up to nature." Though overacting may cause the uneducated to laugh, it "cannot but make the judicious grieve," and one of these outweighs a whole theatre of the others. He has seen actors who "have so strutted and bellowed that I have thought some of Nature's journeymen had made men, and not made them well, they imitated humanity so abominably." This should be completely reformed as well as the license for improvization given to clowns; these should "speak no more than is set down for them" so that they do not obscure "some necessary question of the play" through the laughter of "barren spectators." The players agree and leave to prepare themselves for the performance.

COMMENT: These speeches seem to reflect Shakespeare's own ideas on acting and the drama. He seems to favor a more naturalistic form of acting than was then practiced. This is in line with the theory of drama he inherited from Aristotle which held that "tragedy is an imitation of an action and of life," that is, that it should be true to life. Shakespeare also feels that the play, itself, is more important than the performers, and that the few judicious observers who can understand the play are the playwright's real concern rather than a theatre full of "barren spectators" who simply come to be entertained.

Polonius, Rosencrantz and Guildenstern now enter to tell Hamlet that the King and Qeen will attend the performance, and Hamlet sends them out again to hurry the royal couple.

He now calls Horatio over to him and tells him that he considers him the most just man he has ever met and that, ever since he has been able to distinguish between men, his soul has chosen Horatio to be his truest friend. It is Horatio's Stoicism which most attracts him:

> . . . for thou hast been
> As one in suff'ring all that suffers nothing,
> A man that Fortune's buffets and rewards
> Hast ta'en with equal thanks; and blest are those
> Whose blood and judgement are so well commeddled
> That they are not a pipe for Fortune's finger
> To sound what stop she please.
> Give me that man who is not passion's slave, and
>   I will wear him
> In my heart's core, ay, in my heart of heart,
> As I do thee.

COMMENT: It is clear that Hamlet is attracted to Horatio because he represents opposite qualities from those he, himself, has. Hamlet is one who is "passion's slave," an instrument for "Fortune's finger" to play upon as "she please." He cannot help but admire one like Horatio, therefore, who can accept Fortune's blows without suffering anything. He considers this a blessed condition and hopes that Horatio's presence may help him to control his own nature.

Hamlet reveals that he had earlier confided in Horatio about the circumstances of his father's death. He now continues this by confiding in Horatio his plan about the play soon to be performed. He asks Horatio to help him observe the way Claudius reacts to the part of the play which reenacts his crime and then to compare these observations with his own. He concludes that if Claudius' guilt does not reveal itself under these circumstances then "It is a damned ghost that we have seen, / And my imaginations are as foul / As Vulcan's stithy [smithy]." Horatio agrees and, as the court is now approaching, he tells Horatio to part from him as he must now be "idle." This may refer to the resumption of a mad-man's role.

The King and court enter with a flourish of trumpets and drums. Claudius asks Hamlet how he is and Hamlet answers somewhat obscurely that he is not satisfied with eating promises (a sugges-tion of his disappointed ambition), but Claudius says he cannot make sense of what he is saying. Hamlet now turns to Polonius and asks him about his university acting. Polonius says that he once played Julius Caesar and was killed in the Capitol. (This remark serves as a dramatic foreshadowing of Polonius' fate in the next scene.) The players are now ready to appear and Gertrude asks Hamlet to sit by her. He rejects her, however, saying he prefers the more attractive Ophelia. This supports Polonius' theory as he is quick to point out to Claudius. Hamlet now lies at Ophelia's feet but he treats her with no respect, making several lewd sexual puns (particularly one on "country matters" in which a pun is intended on the first syllable of "country"). These, however, seem to escape Ophelia's understanding. She notes simply that he is "merry." Hamlet replies: "O god, your only jig-maker! What should a man do but be merry?" Since God's creation is a farce, man can do nothing better than to laugh. Both of these points are proven by his mother's behavior: "For look you how cheerfully my mother looks, and my father died within's two hours." When Ophelia objects that "'tis twice two months, my lord," Hamlet ironically returns, "O heavens! die two months ago, and not forgotten yet? Then there's hope a great man's memory may outlive his life half a year." (This is the reference to the time lapse between the first and second acts earlier referred to, at which place the significance of Hamlet's slip that it is two rather than four months since his father's death was explained as revealing that for Hamlet time has really stopped since his encounter with the ghost.)

At this point the players put on the kind of "dumb show" that Hamlet just recently disapproved of in his discussion with them. This "dumb show" silently enacts the plot of the play: a king and queen embrace lovingly; then he lies down in a garden and she leaves. Another man comes in, takes off his crown and kisses it, pours poison in the sleeper's ear and leaves him. The queen re-turns to discover that the king is dead, at which she displays passionate grief. The poisoner returns with some others and they try to comfort her. When the body is carried out, the poisoner woos the queen who, after some harshness, accepts his love.

COMMENT: The question arises as to why Claudius does not react to this clear demonstration of his crime. W. W. Greg first suggested that this proves Claudius innocent of the specific crime recounted to Hamlet by the ghost and that this also disproves the validity of the ghost. John Dover Wilson counters this conclusion with the suggestion, unsupported by any clear reference in the text, that Claudius was probably still arguing with Polonius about the significance of Hamlet's sitting with Ophelia and so did not notice the rapidly performed dumb show. Wilson also argues that the dumb show was not ordered by Hamlet and that he was angered by it, but that it fortunately did no harm. As with Wilson's other theory of the "overheard plot," this makes good dramatic sense though without any textual support. Grebanier suggests that Claudius did recognize the similarity but, with strength of mind, rejected it as a coincidence.

The Player King and Player Queen now enter to begin the play and we are surprised to learn that the major emphasis of the play is not to be on the murder of the king but the infidelity of the queen. The King begins by remembering how long they have been married and the Queen hopes they may continue married just as long, though she is very worried by his recent sickness. He replies that he shall not live long and hopes that she may find as kind a husband as he has been after he dies. She interrupts him, horrified by such a treasonous thought: "In second husband let me be accurst! / None wed the second but who killed the first." In a long reply, the king says that though she may feel that way now, such purposes "like fruit unripe sticks on the tree, / But fall unshaken when they mellow be." In time many things may change her present purposes, for, he concludes: "Our thoughts are ours, their ends none of our own." Nonetheless the queen now makes a powerful vow that she will never remarry, and Hamlet exclaims: "If she should break it now!" He then asks his mother how she likes the play and Gertrude, perhaps with fellow feeling for woman's frailty, replies: "The lady doth protest too much, me thinks." To Hamlet's more serious charge against her in the play, complicity in the murder, she seems, however, quite innocent.

Claudius, apparently aroused by the connection Hamlet seems to be intimating between the Player Queen and Gertrude, now asks Hamlet whether he knows the plot of the play and whether there is any offense in it. Hamlet answers that there is "no offense i' th' world," and, when asked the play's name, that it is called "The Mousetrap." We remember that he had said, "The play's the thing / Wherein I'll catch the conscience of the king," and he now continues to play his little cat-and-mouse game with Claudius by saying that it is the story of a murder committed in Vienna. He then continues: "'Tis a knavish piece of work, but what o' that? Your majesty, and we have free souls, it touches us not." The Player Murderer now enters and Hamlet announces that it is "Lucianus, nephew to the king." When Ophelia comments that he is as good as a stage narrator of the action, Hamlet turns to her and continues his earlier sexual joking with her. He finally calls to the actor playing Lucianus and tells him to begin. The Player King, having in the meantime gone to sleep, Lucianus approaches him, notes the fitness of all things and carefully describes the properties of the poison he is to use. As he pours the poison in the Player King's ear, Hamlet once again starts to explain the story, but Claudius has already risen very upset, as indicated by Gertrude's concern for him, calls for more light, and quickly leaves the hall followed by all except Hamlet and Horatio.

Hamlet reacts to Claudius' breakdown with hysterical glee. He begins to sing and asks Horatio whether this play would not win him a share in a company of players. Horatio calmly answers that he would only earn "half a share" which Hamlet heartly disputes and then continues to sing. As he ends the verse poorly, Horatio again calmly notes, "You might have rhymed." This finally has the effect of dampening Hamlet's high spirits long enough to discuss Claudius' reaction with Horatio and to conclude, "I'll take the ghost's word for a thousand pound."

COMMENT: Although Hamlet had earlier said that he would only write one speech of twelve to sixteen lines, at the end of the performance he seems to claim authorship for the whole scene, and, indeed, there is much about the scene which points to Hamlet's authorship. First, it displays greater preoccupation with the infidelity of the queen than with the murder of the king and seems designed to catch the conscience of his mother as well as of Claudius. Despite the warning of the ghost, Hamlet, as we shall later see, suspects his mother of knowledge of the murder and wishes to test her, a test she passes very well. Secondly, the long speech by the king about "ripeness" and the contrary relationship of will to fate contains ideas which Hamlet is later to embrace as the explanation for his experiences. This speech may represent, then, Hamlet's early testing of these ideas before he is fully ready to affirm them. Thirdly, the relationship of murderer to victim, as Wilson noted, is significantly changed from that of brother to nephew. As this is Hamlet's relationship to Claudius, rather than Claudius' relationship to his brother, the effect of the play in practical terms is to warn Claudius of his intentions. This is, in fact, the meaning which

the rest of the court derives from the play, as we shall see in
the next scene, and may even explain Claudius' disturbance
and so still not prove the ghost's story.

Hamlet's reaction to the performance of the play is so trium-
phant, however, as to suggest something further. Jones
pointed out that as a playwright Hamlet has already accomplished his revenge vicariously through an artistic creation which substituted for reality. We have seen that Hamlet
characteristically releases his destructive impulses through
verbal play. What more natural, then, that as Hamlet sat
down to compose a single speech he should have become so
excited by the various opportunities offered by the play that
he proceeded to rewrite the whole of the first scene up to the
point of the murder, and that when he came to the murder,
itself, something he seemed unable to commit in real life, he
should restructure the murder so that it symbolically represented the very deed he was supposed to perform and could
stand as an artistic fulfillment of this deed. This is certainly
an accepted phenomenon in the case of actual writers and
Shakespeare is perhaps most autobiographical in turning his
princely character into an amateur playwright with a deep
love and knowledge of the theatre.

In continued high spirits, Hamlet calls for some music, asking the
players to bring in the recorders, simple flute-like instruments. At
this point Rosencrantz and Guildenstern enter and desire to talk
with him. They tell him that the King is extremely upset and, as
Hamlet jokes about this with great gaiety, Guildenstern urges him:
"Good my lord, put your discourse into some frame, and start not
so wildly from my affair." Hamlet becomes tamer and Guildenstern
continues his message, that Hamlet's mother "in most great affliction of spirit" has asked him to come to her room to speak with
her before he retires. Hamlet had interrupted this message several
times in the telling until even he apologizes that he cannot make
"a wholesome answer; my wit's deceased."

Rosencrantz now asks him, in virtue of the love Hamlet formerly
had for him, to open his heart to him and tell him the cause of
his diseased mind. Hamlet quickly returns the answer Rosencrantz
has been fishing for in their earlier meeting: "Sir, I lack advancement." When Rosencrantz asks how that can be since he has "the
voice of the King himself for your succession in Denmark," Hamlet
replies with half a proverb which obscurely intimates dissatisfaction
with a long delay. A player enters with the recorders and Hamlet
takes one. He now asks his friends why they are trying to drive
him into a snare. Guildenstern objects that it is just the result of

excessive love. Hamlet then asks Guildenstern to play the recorder for him. Guildenstern says he is unable to play the instrument. After repeated entreaties, Hamlet finally says: "Why, look you now, how unworthy a thing you make of me! You would play upon me, you would seem to know my stops, you would pluck out the heart of my mystery, you would sound me from my lowest note to the top of my compass; and there is much music, excellent voice, in this little organ, yet cannot you make it speak." Polonius now enters to tell Hamlet again that his mother wishes to speak to him and immediately. Hamlet, however, proceeds to have fun at his expense. He asks Polonius whether he sees a cloud shaped like a camel. When Polonius agrees, Hamlet changes his mind and says he thinks it looks first like a weasel and then like a whale with Polonius agreeing each time. Finally, he tells Polonius that he will come to his mother soon. In an "aside" he says, "They fool me to the top of my bent," and then asks them all to leave him.

COMMENT: Hamlet's state of mind after the play has been genuinely unsettled, as Guildenstern points out and Hamlet agrees, but he then consciously puts on his mad pose for Polonius. He is, finally, thoroughly tired of all of them, of their hypocritical attempts to "fool" him and of his attempts to fool and befuddle them. But, though he despises them for their attempts to "pluck out the heart of my mystery," he is no closer to understanding the real cause of his diseased mind than they.

Worn out by all the "fooling" with Rosencrantz, Guildenstern and Polonius and committed to visit his mother, Hamlet's mood now changes. Left alone in depressed spirits after his recent hysteria, he notes:

> 'Tis now the very witching time of night,
> When churchyards yawn, and hell itself breathes out
> Contagion to this world. Now could I drink hot blood
> And do such bitter business as the day
> Would quake to look on.

As he is going in this murderous mood to visit his mother, he tells his heart not to lose its natural feelings for her however cruelly he may act: "I will speak daggers to her, but use none." He then exits.

COMMENT: It is interesting, first, that the call to visit his mother brings out murderous feelings in him despite her recently proven innocence, and, secondly, that he sees such murderous impulses in the context of "hell" and the contagious disease it spreads. It is also interesting that when

Hamlet believes the ghost to have been vindicated by his play, his mind becomes diseased and that he now feels himself to be in power of hell. His primary concern at this point is to keep himself from murdering his mother; he seems to have completely forgotten about Claudius.

SUMMARY Hamlet dominates this scene and reveals the following things about himself:

1. His understanding, love and talent for the theatre are shown by his advice to the players, the play he writes, and his delight with the performance.

2. He seems to be enjoying the game of espionage that he and everyone else is playing: he tests his mother as well as Claudius, bringing Horatio in to help him with the latter; and he throws out clues to everyone interested in the cause of his own disorder—he suggests to Claudius, directly, through the play and through his agents Rosencrantz and Guildenstern, that the cause is frustrated ambition, and he arouses Polonius and perhaps his mother through his exhibitionistic attentions to Ophelia.

3. He makes a decisive choice with regards to all his associates. He chooses to accept Horatio as his bosom companion and he rejects all others. He treats Ophelia as though she were an indecent woman, and becomes thoroughly fed up with Rosencrantz, Guildenstern and Polonius.

4. He undergoes various changes of mood from complete seriousness at the beginning with the players and with Horatio to growing hysterical high spirits throughout the performance of the play and especially after its close, to a final murderous seriousness as he leaves for his mother's chamber.

ACT III: SCENE 3

The King is seen talking to Rosencrantz and Guildenstern in a room of the castle about the danger which Hamlet's madness poses to him. He informs them that he is dispatching them to go with Hamlet to England. Guildenstern says that the danger of regicide represents a "most holy and religious fear" to the very many people who depend upon the King, who "live and feed upon your majesty." Rosencrantz continues that a king is more obligated to protect himself than a private person since the welfare of many lives depend upon him. He compares the death of a king to a whirlpool which draws "what's near it with it," then to a huge wheel fixed on the summit of the highest mountain "to whose huge spokes ten thousand lesser things" are joined which attend "the boist'rous ruin" when it falls. He concludes: "Never alone / Did the king sigh, but with a general groan." The King now tells them to hasten their preparations for the journey which will imprison the cause of "this fear" and they leave to attend to this.

> **COMMENT:**   The remarks of the courtiers reflect the general Renaissance belief in "the Divine Right of Kings," which James I, shortly after the writing of *Hamlet,* presented as a formal decree. This doctrine holds that kings are divinely established to ensure the welfare of their subjects and that regicide, the murder of a king, is therefore not only a political crime but a religious sin. Claudius again makes use of this doctrine in Act IV: Scene 5, as we shall see, when he says that divinity protects a king from treasonous acts. The effect the presentation of this doctrine has upon the play is to place Hamlet's proposed revenge in a still more serious light, not merely as the sin of murder but of regicide. Though it is true that Claudius himself committed regicide, he is now the anointed king and the horror of regicide, which an Elizabethan audience would have felt most keenly, attends him as much as it formerly did Hamlet, Sr.

Polonius now enters to tell Claudius that Hamlet is going to his mother's room and that he is now also going there to hide himself in her room.

Left alone, Claudius gives way to the guilt which is beginning to torment him despite all his practical efforts to protect himself. We saw it earlier in his reaction to a chance remark by Polonius about hypocrisy and then in his reaction to the play. Now he cries out: "O, my offense is rank, it smells to heaven; / It hath the primal eldest curse upon't, / A brother's murther." The curse of Cain, who killed his brother Abel in the first biblical murder, was alienation from God. This is now the condition of Clauduis, for he says: "Pray can I not, / Though inclination be as sharp as will. / My stronger guilt defeats my strong intent." But then he asks himself what the purpose of divine mercy is if not to forgive the guilty. Feeling more hopeful, he now asks himself what form of prayer he can use. He realizes that he cannot simply ask God to "forgive me my foul murther," since he still possesses the results "for which I did the murther, / My crown, mine own ambition, and my queen." Though it may be possible in this "corrupted" world to be pardoned while still retaining the fruits of crime, he is fully aware that " 'tis not so above. / There is no shuffling; there the action lies / In his true nature." Aware that he cannot be divinely pardoned and so be relieved of his guilt while he still enjoys the ful-

fillment of his royal ambition and the possession of his beloved
Queen, he realizes that his only remaining possibility of pardon
is to "try what repentance can," though such repentance would
involve his giving up of the worldly happiness he has derived from
his crown and Queen. He knows that such repentance could effect
his pardon, yet is still in despair because he is too much in love
with his crown and Queen to give them up: "Yet what can it
when one cannot repent? / O wretched state! O bosom black as
death! / O limèd soul, that struggling to be free / Art more engaged!" And yet the despair of his guilt is so great that he finally
does pray to receive the grace which would enable him to give up
the beloved effects of his crime and achieve true repentance: "Help,
angels! Make assay. / Bow stubborn knees, and, heart with strings
of steel, / Be soft as sinews of the new-born babe. / All may be
well." He kneels in such a deeply engrossed state of desperate
prayer that he does not hear Hamlet's entrance.

When we last saw Hamlet, his mother's invitation to visit her had
put him in a murderous rage against her which he was trying to
control. Now on his way to his mother's room, as Polonius has
recently informed us, he accidentally comes upon Claudius alone
and in prayer. He realizes that this is a perfect opportunuity to
perform the revenge, especially as his conscience is now clear as to
Claudius' guilt (based on Claudius' reaction to the play) and as
he has already been informed (as he tells his mother in the next
scene) that he must leave immediately for England. His threatening
behavior to the King, both in the scenes with Ophelia and with the
the play, have thoroughly aroused Claudius to take precautions
against him so that, if he does not perform the revenge now, he
may never again have as good an opportunity. Seeing his opportunity, Hamlet says: "Now might I do it pat, now 'a is a-praying, /
And now I'll do't." But his use of the word "might" already shows
his lack of inclination to kill Claudius now, for his whole spirit is
eagerly bent on his coming confrontation with his mother, and so he
finds an immediate excuse to delay his revenge: "And so 'a goes
to heaven, / Am so am I revenged. That would be scanned." It is
not religious scruples which prevent him from killing a man in the
pious act of prayer, but the thought that, as Claudius is purging his
soul, he would go to heaven upon death whereas his father's soul
was unprepared for death and so went to purgatory. Unsatisfied
simply to perform earthly justice, Hamlet wants his revenge to have
eternal effects and he therefore wants to ensure Claudius' damnation as well as death. It is with this thought that he puts away his
drawn sword:

> Up, sword, and know thou a more horrid hent
>   [occasion].
> When he is drunk asleep, or in his rage,

Or in th' incestuous pleasure of his bed,
At game a-swearing, or about some act
That has no relish of salvation in't—
Then trip him, that his heels may kick at heaven,
And that his soul may be as damned and black
As hell, whereto it goes.

Looking forward to this more horrid occasion and also to seeing his mother who has been waiting for him during this unfortunate delay ("My mother stays"), he leaves the room. Claudius now rises to reveal that his prayer has not been effective, that he has not been truly able to repent: "My words fly up, my thoughts remain below. / Words without thoughts never to heaven go."

COMMENT AND SUMMARY: In this scene the ethical stature of the two leading characters has been reversed. As Claudius kneels in desperate prayer for the religious strength to give up his crown and Queen in true repentance, there is little doubt that at that moment he is ethically superior to the dark figure standing above him with drawn sword whose only reason for not committing murder is that such murder would not be horrible enough to satisfy his vengeance. Hamlet's vengeance here goes beyond the requirements of even the honor code, which is only concerned with the overcoming of earthly sin through the execution of earthly justice. Nowhere else is Hamlet so fully infected by the power of hell which "breathes out contagion to this world." But as this power is fully directed at this moment against his mother, it simply provides a devilish excuse to end this unforseen delay to its true purposes.

In following personal inclination rather than policy at this moment, however, Hamlet is placing himself at a fatal disadvantage with regards to Claudius, the master intriguer. All of Hamlet's mad behavior and intrigues have led him to this moment of necessary action. His misuse of this moment now allows Claudius' plan to send him away from Elsinore to take effect. No further opportunity will arise for Hamlet to take revenge without also losing his own life.

The final irony of the scene is that even Hamlet's expressed reason for the delay, the effectiveness of Claudius' prayer, proves to be invalid and that he could have achieved his evil wish to send Claudius' soul to hell. From the religious perspective of Hamlet's own soul, if not his life, it is well, however, that he did not perform his revenge at this time, for though he might have survived the murder, his spiritual state at the time he committed the murder would have damned his own soul to hell.

ACT III: SCENE 4

We are now in Gertrude's room in the castle. Polonius, alone with
Gertrude, tells her that Hamlet will be there immediately and that
she should be very forceful with him, should tell him that she has
protected him as much as she could but that his behavior has been
too unrestrained to be endured any longer. Polonius now withdraws
behind a hanging tapestry as Hamlet is heard approaching.

He enters and immediately asks his mother "what's the matter?"
She answers: "Hamlet, thou hast thy father much offended." Offended by this reference to Claudius as his father, he sharply returns: "Mother, you have my father much offended." The
conversation quickly proceeds with Gertrude objecting to Hamlet's
"idle tongue" and Hamlet objecting to her "wicked tongue," until
she finally asks, "Have you forgot me?" Though she is asking
Hamlet whether he has forgotten the respect due to a mother, he
answers with a bitter identification: "You are the queen, your
husband's brother's wife, / And (would it were not so) you are my
mother."

Seeing that she will not get anywhere with him, she proposes to
end their meeting, but Hamlet is not going to let this longed for
opportunity to speak his mind to his mother get away from him so
easily. Forcing her angrily to sit down, his expression must appear
to her so murderous that she is forced to cry out in terror for help:
"What wilt thou do? Thou wilt not murther me? Help, ho!" At this
the startled Polonius also begins to cry for help and Hamlet, quickly
drawing his sword, drives it through the tapestry killing the figure
behind it with the words: "How now? a rat? Dead for a ducat,
dead!" The Queen cries out to ask him what he has done and
Hamlet replies, "Nay, I know not. Is it the King?"

COMMENT: In the next scene, Gertrude describes what
happened in the following words, which are best discussed
here: "Mad as the sea and wind when both contend / Which
is the mightier. In his lawless fit, / Behind the arras [tapestry]
hearing something stir, / Whips out his rapier, cries, 'A rat,
a rat!' / And in this brainish apprehension kills / The unseen
good old man." There is little doubt that this is a good description of what actually happened, that Hamlet, as he says,
did not "know" what he was doing because he was tempo-
rarily insane.

That Hamlet truly felt murderous as he was coming to his
mother's room is proven by the fact that within a few minutes
in her room he does commit murder. That this murderous

impulse was not directed at Claudius is proven by the fact that he does not take advantage of his opportunity to kill Claudius even though everything points to the necessity for doing so but quickly rationalizes away this chance to murder Claudius so as not to further delay his coming to his mother. That the murderous impulse is directed at his mother is proven, first by the need he feels to control himself against murdering her ("Let me be cruel, not unnatural; / I will speak daggers to her, but use none."), and secondly by his mother's terror for her life as she looks at his expression seconds before he murders.

What must have happened, then, is that the murderous impulse towards his mother so overpowered his reason as he physically forced her to sit, that he was on the point of murdering her when another sound distracted his attention from her long enough for his will to reassert itself and deflect the intended blow from his mother onto the nearest object. His temporary insanity at this moment is clearly shown by his incoherent cry which accompanies the murder: "How now? a rat? Dead for a ducat, dead!" At the moment when he murders he does not know what he is doing, only what he must not do, that he must not murder his mother. At this moment of murderous rage at his mother's infidelity, however, he hears the sound of an intruder in his mother's bedroom when she was supposed to be alone with him and, associating all such intruders as the lowest vermin, he vents his wrath upon it. It is only after the deed is done that he associates the intruding "rat" with Claudius and hopes that he may have actually accomplished his long delayed revenge without having planned it. That this hope is only an afterthought rather than the motive of his deed is proven by the fact that he had just left Claudius kneeling in prayer as he was on his way to his mother's room and so he could not have expected Claudius to have gotten to his mother's room before him, as, indeed, would have been impossible.

The Queen well describes the act when she exclaims: "O, what a rash and bloody deed is this!" But Hamlet is still more concerned to attack his mother than to care about what he has done, and he immediately replies with his worst accusation against her: "A bloody deed—almost as bad, good mother, / As kill a king, and marry with his brother." The Queen is innocently shocked and confused by the meaning of such a suggestion—"As kill a King?"—and so Hamlet, simply repeating "Ay, lady, it was my word," drops the subject. He then lifts the tapestry and, seeing it is Polonius, reacts only with a casual coldness which becomes a bit mocking: "Thou wretched, rash, intruding fool, farewell! / I took thee for thy

better. Take thy fortune. / Thou find'st to be too busy is some
danger." Then, imediately dismissing the whole subject, he returns
to his primary object of attacking his mother with verbal daggers
and says to her: "Leave wringing of your hands. Peace, sit you
down / And let me wring your heart."

When the Queen asks what she can have done to deserve such rudeness from him, Hamlet begins to describe in fierce terms the im-
modesty, hypocrisy and irreligiousness with which she has debased
her "marriage vows." He then tells her to compare the pictures
of her two husbands and asks: "Have you eyes? / Could you on
this fair mountain leave to feed, / And batten on this moor?" Not
only was his father far superior to Claudius but she cannot even
excuse her change as resulting from love since she is too old, he
claims, to be capable of such romantic feelings. Her behavior is
so lacking in sense that it must be the work of a "devil" who has
so blinded her that she has lost all sense of shame. And as he
continues to cry out against her lack of shame, she finally begs him
to "speak no more" for he is turning her eyes inward to look upon
the guilt in her soul which she cannot erase. The admission of her
guilt only inspires Hamlet to make his most revolting description
of her act: "Nay, but to live / In the rank sweat of an enseamèd
[greasy] bed, / Stewed in corruption, honeying and making love /
Over the nasty sty—" Once more she interrupts him to beg him to
stop tormenting her with "these words like daggers." But he continues until he forces a third anguished cry, "No more."

At this point the ghost reappears, this time dressed in his nightgown
rather than his armor, and Hamlet is stopped from the relentless
and increasing fury of his attack upon his already crying mother.
Calling for angelic protection, he asks the "gracious figure" of the
ghost if he has come to "chide" his "tardy son" for having let his
"dread command" become "lapsed in time and passion." The ghost
agrees that this is why he has had to return: 'This visitation /
Is but to whet they blunted purpose." But, as Gertrude is looking upon
Hamlet's conversation with "amazement," having already said,
"Alas, he's mad," the ghost tells Hamlet to "speak to her." To his
question as to how she feels, she responds with concern for him since
he seems to be talking to nothing. Hamlet points to the ghost and
describes for her his pitiful expression but she can neither see nor
hear anything unusual. At this point the ghost "steals away" out
of the door and, as Hamlet continues to describe the ghost's last
motions, Gertrude concludes that what he has seen must have been
a hallucination produced by his own brain, such hallucinations
being a special effect of madness. Hamlet denies that he is mad
and, as proof, says that he can repeat everything he has said. Then,
fearing he is to lose the whole effect of his earlier tirade, he tells

her that she should not flatter her soul that it is his madness which has magnified her sins for this will only increase her corruption.

COMMENT: The reappearance of the ghost at this point has been puzzling to most critics. Is this the same objective ghost as before or is Gertrude right that it is a hallucination? If this is a hallucination, does this cast doubt on the earlier ghost as perhaps a product of group hysteria? If this is an objective ghost and the same one as earlier, what is the meaning of Gertrude's inability to see it? Is it that her innocence protects her from seeing a diabolic agent, or is it her guilt which has alienated her from the sight of her abused husband's ghost or of an angel? As for the ghost being produced by Hamlet's madness, Hamlet had earlier suggested that his melancholy may have attracted diabolic interest to undertake the ghostly impersonation as a means of damning him and his mind has been nowhere as diseased as in his recent murder. Although Hamlet speaks sanely enough after the ghost's exit in his compelling need to prove his sanity to his mother, he was becoming quite agitated again before the ghost's entrance. Does the ghost reappear at this point to prevent a possible second murder attempt upon Gertrude? Does this prove that the ghost is the genuine spirit of Hamlet, Sr., that he returns out of love for his wife, tries to shield her from any disturbance and leaves broken hearted at her failure to perceive him? Or is the ghost simply a figment produced by Hamlet's own growing guilt over his preoccupation with his mother's sins which, as he immediately explains as the ghost's reason for appearing, has caused his "passion" for revenge to lapse even at the most opportune moment and when he could no longer excuse his delay with doubt? Shakespeare does not provide us with sufficient means for answering all of these questions. Indeed, he seems more concerned to raise these final questions about the ghost than to answer them, to keep the nature of the ghost ambiguous. The effect of the ghost's appearance, however, is clear. It does serve to calm Hamlet's spirit at a point where he is becoming agitated once more and to make Hamlet consciously aware of his misdirected efforts. (This will be further discussed in the Summary to this scene.) The ghost had earlier told Hamlet that he should "leave her to heaven" rather than attempt to punish her. Now Hamlet does return to this more proper attitude.

Attempting to turn his mother's spirit back to her former purity, he advises her to do what Claudius had earlier himself attempted: "Confess yourself to heaven, / Repent what's past, avoid what is to come, / And do not spread the compost on the weeds / To

make them ranker." Calmer now and feeling sorry for his former
rudeness to her, he asks her to "forgive me this my virtue." But
then, excusing himself by the needs of a corrupt time, he again
shows a touch of self-righteous disrespect when he concludes that
"Virtue itself of vice must pardon beg, / Yea, curb and woo for
leave to do him good."

But Hamlet has achieved his wish; he has caused his mother to
contritely admit her guilt to him as she now does in saying, "O
Hamlet, thou hast cleft my heart in twain." Happy with his success,
he tells her to "throw away the worser part of it" by never again
going to his uncle's bed. By way of farewell, he says: "Once more,
good night, / And when you are desirous to be blest, / I'll blessing
beg of you."

> **COMMENT:** For months Hamlet has felt himself wronged
> by his mother's remarriage. Now that Hamlet has returned
> the injury to her, has made her cringe in torment under his
> dagger words and admit her guilt to him, he is able to achieve
> an emotional reconciliation with her. As she begs him for
> forgiveness, he can do the same to her and they can both
> kneel down for blessing to each other. Shakespeare is to
> repeat this mode of parent-child reconciliation in *King Lear*
> when King Lear says to Cordelia, the daughter he disin-
> herited: "Come, let's away to prison. / We two alone will sing
> like birds i' th' cage. / When thou dost ask me blessing, I'll
> kneel down / And ask of thee forgiveness."

In this moment of harmonious reconciliation with his mother, Hamlet achieves a sense of general well-being and harmony with the
universe which enables him to view his murder of Polonius in a
new light. Noticing the dead body of Polonius for the first time
since the murder, he says:

> For this same lord, I do repent; but heaven hath
>   pleased it so,
> To punish me with this, and this with me,
> That I must be their scourge and minister.

> **COMMENT:** This is the first time that Hamlet has expressed
> his harmony with heaven's purposes. Earlier he believed his de-
> sires for suicide and revenge to be opposed by heaven, had
> viewed the whole of creation as a sterile "quintessence of
> dust" and God as a maker of farces. Now he accepts the
> murder of Polonius and its consequences for himself as being
> the will of heaven and sees himself in a new role as heaven's
> "scourge and minister." Although he had accepted his role

of revenger from the first as a means of achieving the reformation of his society, the murder it involved had seemed religiously forbidden and had involved him in a conflict between the honor code and religious commandments. Now the two seem to have become joined for him. The question arises as to why he should have experienced this general reorientation at this time and in relation to the murder of Polonius and what its significance is for the play as a whole.

One immediate explanation is the one mentioned above, the spreading out of his harmonious reconciliation with his mother to embrace the whole of creation. Though this may explain his acceptance of the will of heaven, how is the act, itself, to be explained as the work of heaven? An answer to this may be provided by the Queen's statement that his deed was "rash." Not only was the deed unpremeditated, but Hamlet seemed not to "know" what he was doing. But if the murder he accomplished while beside himself was a good deed, then some other intelligence, which could only have been divine, must have directed it. The question now arises as to how Hamlet could view the accomplished fact of Polonius' death as good, in fact, as divinely desired. To this point we already have Hamlet's words to the dead Polonius: "Thou find'st to be too busy is some danger." And what was this "wretched, rash, intruding fool" busying himself about if not the evil business of the adulterous regicide who had thrown the time "out of joint" and whose evil he had already vowed himself to "scourge," to punish as with a whip. He now sees that he was divinely appointed not only to kill Claudius but also to destroy all those to whom his evil influence has extended and, as we shall see, this is soon to include Rosencrantz and Guildenstern. While Hamlet might just as well have construed the deed as the result of diabolic possession, indeed, he felt himself so possessed as he went to his mother's room, he never considers this possibility. He has, instead, that sense of inner conviction, which might also be termed "conversion," that he has received ordination as heaven's "scourge and minister." To ask why this should be takes us onto somewhat more shaky ground.

Certainly Hamlet detests Polonius both for his stupidity and his hypocritical conniving. He is soon to treat Polonius' body in a most contemptuous fashion and to call him "a foolish prating knave." He has never missed an opportunity to make contemptuous fun of him and his satire has often been directed at Polonius' relationship to his daughter. Here we may see a further motive for Hamlet's dislike of Polonius, his suspicion that Polonius may be responsible for Ophelia's rejection of him, that Polonius was as much an interloper in Hamlet's own love relationship with Ophelia as Polonius had just been in his mother's bedroom. The satiric daggers Hamlet had earlier thrust at Polonius have now found their emotional fulfillment in the accidental murder of the man Hamlet detests as fully if not more than he does Claudius, and this inner satisfaction supports the sense of cosmic harmony which his reconciliation with his mother had produced in him. Though consciously he repents the accident both because he cannot consider his grounds against Polonius sufficient to justify his planned destruction and because this killing will make his actual task of revenge more difficult to accomplish, he is so far from denying his satisfaction with the result that the death of this hated "counsellor" of his enemy seems to him part of a cosmic plan to scourge the evil of the Danish court.

This is perhaps sufficient explanation, certainly as far as the actual text can take us, but the psychoanalytic interpretation does provide us with an interesting further hypothesis here. We remember that Ernest Jones, following Freud's earlier suggestion, had elaborated the theory that Hamlet has an "Oedipus Complex." In line with this, Jones suggests that Hamlet subconsciously views Polonius as a father substitute and that his expressed hatred of Polonius is really the expression of his repressed hatred for his own father, also an interloper between his mother and himself. His satisfaction with the murder of Polonius, then, reflects his subconscious sense of fulfillment of the repressed Oedipal desire to murder his father.

There is much in the text to support Jones' suggestion that Hamlet subconsciously identifies Polonius with his father. In Act II: Scene 2, Hamlet had directed his most vicious satire against Polonius' old age: "Slanders, sir, for the satirical rogue says here that old men have grey beards." In Act I: Scene 2, moreover, the first mark of identification of the ghost with his father that Hamlet asks of Horatio is the following: "His beard was grizzled [grey], no?" Hamlet's father also was an old man, and what further similarity he may have had with Polonius may be guessed from the fact that Polonius' present position in the court is so high because he was apparently the most intimate counselor of the former King, Hamlet, Sr. In fact, the possible similarity of Hamlet, Sr., to Polonius, which Hamlet has never admitted to his conscious mind, may help to explain Gertrude's adultery with her husband's younger brother. Certainly Hamlet's view of both his mother's love relationships has not been accurate; the relationship of his parents was not as ideal as he had imagined and, from what we know and are to learn of Claudius' devotion to Gertrude, this new relationship of his mother can hardly be considered simply as "stewed in corruption, honeying and making love over the nasty sty." As Jones and other commentators have pointed out, Hamlet's obsession with sexual corruption, both in this scene and elsewhere, is hardly normal.

Whatever Hamlet's subconscious feelings about the murder of Polonius may be, there is no doubt, however, that Hamlet's accidental murder of Polonius marks the turning point in the play, both in terms of Hamlet's external situation and of his spiritual orientation: this act places him in the power of Claudius but it also gives him his sense of ordination as heaven's "scourge and minister."

Hamlet excuses the fatal effects of his new role by saying, "I must be cruel only to be kind." He says that he will take the body from the room and "will answer well the death I gave him." Aware that "worse remains behind" for him as a result of this killing, he prepares to say goodnight again but then remembers to tell his mother that she should not "let the bloat king" for "a pair of reechy kisses" cause her to confess that Hamlet is not truly mad "but mad in craft." Gertrude promises this and then Hamlet reminds her that, as she knows, he must leave for England. He now confides in her that he neither trusts the sealed letters Claudius is sending nor his "two schoolfellows," Rosencrantz and Guildenstern, whom Claudius is also sending along with him: "They bear the mandate; they must sweep my way / And marshall me to knavery." With his new sense of divine mission, however, Hamlet is not worried for his own safety and success:

> Let it work.
> For 'tis the sport to have the enginer
> Hoise with his own petar [mine], and't shall go hard
> But I will delve one yard below their mines
> And blow them at the moon. O, 'tis most sweet
> When in one line two crafts directly meet.

So far from being worried, Hamlet is elated with the thought that he will somehow turn against his former friends the evil that they are now helping Claudius to work against himself. He feels no sympathy for any of Claudius' accomplices. Seeing Polonius only as a means of getting himself shipped off to England, he says most crudely: "This man shall set me packing. / I'll lug the guts into the neighbor room." Then, calling Polonius "a foolish prating knave" and saying a final goodnight to his mother, he leaves the room tugging the body of Polonius after him.

SUMMARY This scene is the turning point in the play for the following reasons:

1. After having missed his opportunity to murder Claudius, Hamlet's "rash and bloody" accidental killing of Polonius makes it impossible for either Hamlet or his mother to delay Claudius' purpose to send him away to England. This makes his own task of revenge more difficult.

2. The effect of this deed, as we shall see in Act IV: Scene 3, is to make Claudius' purpose in sending him to England more deadly. Hamlet has not only made his revenge more difficult but placed his life in danger.

3. The accidental killing of Polonius works a drastic change in Hamlet's nature. This violent act, the result of two months of mounting tension, marks the end of his downward spiritual progress and the beginning of a more positive spiritual movement. If the first appearance of the ghost caused a hellish state of spiritual alienation from God which reached its most extreme form in Hamlet's diabolic reasons for not killing Claudius and his equally thoughtless killing of Polonius minutes later, the appearance of the "gracious figure" of the ghost in this scene begins to effect his reconciliation to divine purposes. This suggests that the ghost's nature may, itself, have changed and this for one of two reasons. Either this is his father's spirit come from purgatory, as it earlier claimed, and the effects of purgatory are beginning to be seen in the purging of his formerly evil desire for selfish revenge and its replacement by a new sense of divine justice; or these are two different ghostly impersonations, the former by a devil and the latter by an angel. In any case, Hamlet is now animated by a new sense of identification with divine justice just as earlier he had been moved by his alienation from it.

ACT IV: SCENES 1, 2, 3

The King and Queen, with Rosencrantz and Guildenstern, enter another room of the castle soon after the killing of Polonius. Claudius asks Gertrude why she is sighing so heavily and, after asking Rosencrantz and Guildenstern to leave them alone a while, she answers with a description of Hamlet's "mad" killing of Polonius.

After a brief statement of sorrow, "O heavy deed!," Claudius immediately sees the danger Hamlet's action poses to him:

> It had been so with us, had we been there.
> His liberty is full of threats to all,
> To you yourself, to us, to every one.
> Alas, how shall this bloody deed be answered?
> It will be laid to us.

Not only might Hamlet have killed either himself or Gertrude in place of Polonius, but he might yet do so if he is not immediately restrained. Even as it is, he is afraid that he, himself, will be blamed for the murder and rightly so, for it was his "love" which prevented him from truly recognizing the danger earlier. Asking Gertrude where Hamlet is, she tells him that he has gone to draw away the body and, now sorry for his deed, "weeps for what is done." Claudius now tells Gertrude that he must ship Hamlet away by dawn and then must use his utmost skill to excuse the dead. He calls back Rosencrantz and Guildenstern, tells them of Hamlet's action and that they should find him, speak politely to him and bring the body into the chapel. After they leave, he tells Gertrude that they must also go and tell the council what has happened and what he means to do with Hamlet so as to offset any possible rumors that may arise. Very disturbed by this situation, he says as they leave, "My soul is full of discord and dismay."

In the second scene, Rosencrantz and Guildenstern come upon Hamlet just after he has hidden the body of Polonius. Hamlet's attitude throughout the next two scenes is viciously satirical, though his satire is primarily a reaction to his renewed awareness of death through contact with Polonius' body. To their question as to what he has done with the body, Hamlet replies that he has "compounded it with dust." As they insist upon knowing, Hamlet objects to being "demanded of a sponge," and he explains this reference by saying: "Ay, sir, that soaks up the king's countenance, his rewards, his authorities. But such officers do the king best service in the end. He keeps them, like an ape, in the corner of his jaw, first mouthed, to be last swallowed. When he needs what you have gleaned, it is but squeezing you and, sponge, you shall be dry again." Hamlet satirically tells them that they have lost all human identity by selling their services to the King and that the only reward they may expect for selling their souls is to be destroyed by the King who uses them, but they claim not to understand him. After continuing his contemptuous satire against both them and the body for a bit longer, he demands to be brought to the King and they all leave to go to Claudius.

The third scene begins with Claudius' explanations to some of his advisers. He tells them that he has sent for Hamlet since it is dangerous to let Hamlet continue to go about "loose" but that he must not "put the strong law on him" and "he's loved of the distracted multitude." All he can do, therefore, is to send Hamlet immediately away while giving the impression that this has been done with much deliberation. Rosencrantz now enters to say that they have been unable to find where Hamlet has put the body but that they have brought him guarded to the King and that he is waiting outside the room. Claudius orders Hamlet's appearance and, when he enters, immediately demands of Hamlet to be told where Polonius is. Hamlet satirically answers that Polonius is "at supper," and then, when questioned about this, explains that this supper is "Not where he eats, but where 'a is eaten. A certain convocation of politic worms are e'en at him. Your worm is your only emperor for diet. We fat all creatures else to fat us, and we fat ourselves for maggots. Your fat king and your lean beggar is but variable service—two dishes, but to one table. That's the end."

COMMENT: In Act III: Scene 3, Guildenstern had described the courtiers' dependence upon the King by using the image of eating; he had said that they "feed upon your majesty." In Act IV: Scene 2, Hamlet had said to Rosencrantz and Guildenstern that the King keeps courtiers like themselves "in the corner of his jaw, first mouthed, to be last swallowed." Such images conjure up a vision of a jungle in which the animals are engaged in eating each other. In other words, we are being told through images that the court is really a dog-eat-dog world. Not only is ambition described in this fashion but also such other "appetites" as sensual lust. Hamlet had asked his mother in Act III: Scene 4, "Could you on this fair mountain leave to feed,/And batten on this moor?" And in Act IV: Scene 1, Claudius had compared his "love," which kept him from imprisoning Hamlet, to a "foul disease" which he allowed to "feed / Even on the pith of life." Love then, is a diseased appetite which feeds either on oneself or on another. The ironic conclusion to this picture of humanity as the prey to animal appetites is now given in the speech by Hamlet in which he says that the result of all this feeding is simply to fatten ourselves for worms and that no position in this world can protect a man from the final appetite of death. Such a vision of the world is close to that of Hamlet's first soliloquy, in which he said: "How weary, stale, flat, and unprofitable / Seem to me all the uses of this world! / Fie on't, ah, fie, 'tis an unweeded garden / That grows to seed. Things rank and gross in nature / Possess it merely." The world is composed of "rank and gross" animals feeding upon one another for the "unprofitable" end of feeding worms.

From this study of the imagery, however, we can see that such a sentiment is not simply Hamlet's, although he is its best and most frequent spokesman, but also Shakespeare's, for the pattern of feeding imagery is contributed to by other characters besides Hamlet. This is to be considered, then, as the objective vision of reality in this play. Hamlet is more perceptive than others insofar as he sees something of the whole pattern, and his problem, as we shall see more fully in his next soliloquy, is to determine what action is demanded of him in the face of such a reality.

Hamlet continues to discuss the conversion of men to worms to fish to men again until Claudius finally demands of him "Where is Polonius?" To this Hamlet flippantly answers: "In heaven. Send thither to see. If your messenger find him not there, seek him i' th' other place yourself. But if indeed you find him not within this month, you shall nose him as you go up, the stairs into the lobby."

After sending attendants to find the body of Polonius, Claudius informs Hamlet that "for thine especial safety," he is to leave immediately for England. To this Hamlet says "Good," and Claudius adds, "So is it, if thou knew'st our purposes." Hamlet does see through Claudius' false mask of goodwill, however, as he indicates by his ambiguous reply, 'I see a cherub that sees them.' Feeling heaven to be on his side, he is not overly worried, and, after another bit of verbal quibbling, he leaves to prepare himself for England.

Left alone, Claudius reveals that his letter to the King of England demands "the present death of Hamlet." This alone can cure the feverish anxiety which Hamlet's free raging produces in him and which prevents his enjoying his fortune. The scene now ends as Claudius leaves the stage.

COMMENT AND SUMMARY: We are not told whether Claudius' original purpose in sending Hamlet to England was to effect his death or whether this is a new purpose resulting from Hamlet's killing of Polonius. The evidence of the play would seem to argue, however, that Claudius wrote a new letter after he learned of Hamlet's killing. Had he already planned this in his earlier letter to England, there should have been some mention of this when Claudius was unburdening his guilt to heaven. Since at that time the only sin upon Claudius' conscience was his murder of his brother and since this single sin was so tormenting his conscience, it is difficult to believe that he would want to add a new sin to his con-

science or that, if he did, his conscience would have been
free of it.

Once Hamlet has killed, however, it is clear to Claudius that
he can no longer allow his squeamish conscience to further
endanger himself. What is more, Hamlet's behavior to him
is so tormenting that, after having allowed him complete
liberty for four months to say or do anything while himself
exercising complete self-restraint in Hamlet's presence,
Claudius is finally at the breaking point and can endure
Hamlet's taunting existence no more. Hamlet, for his part,
has done everything to antagonize Claudius and break his
composure. He has, indeed, been more concerned to make
Claudius squirm than actually to murder him. But Hamlet's
very success in making Claudius squirm, in getting under his
skin, has destroyed Claudius' original good intentions towards
him with the final result that Claudius now means to cause
Hamlet's death. Claudius had hoped that one murder would
solve all his problems and he had delayed longer than he
should have even considering the necessity of a new murder.
When he does, however, he can no longer actually commit
the murder himself and delegates this task to another.

While Hamlet has been throwing Claudius' soul into "discord
and dismay" with its final murderous decision, Hamlet, himself, has shown nothing of the repentent reaction to his
killing that Gertrude mentions. Instead, he continues to
cavort in a most unseemly fashion, making a gay game out
of hiding the body. Despite this new theological insight, he
is in the same hysterical state as he was at the close of the
play within the play and little changed from the way he was
at the first. His psychological distress has thus far only resulted in an unnecessary death and his own mortal danger.

ACT IV: SCENE 4

The scene opens the following morning on a road near the Danish
border. Fortinbras enters with his army and stops to talk to his
Captain. He tells the Captain to go to the Danish King with his
greetings and to remind him of the permission he had earlier granted
Fortinbras to transport a Norwegian army over Danish territory.
The Captain agrees to do this and is left alone on stage after the
departure of Fortinbras and the army. Hamlet now enters with
Rosencrantz, Guildenstern and others on their way to the ship
which is to bear them to England. He questions the Captain as to

the nature and purpose of the army and is told that it is a Norwegian army commanded by Fortinbras on its way to conquer a
small piece of Polish land "that hath in it no profit but the name."
When Hamlet suggests that the Poles then "never will defend it,"
he is told that "it is already garrisoned." Hamlet now comments
that the expenditure of "two thousand souls and twenty thousand
ducats" over "the question of this straw" is the sick result of "much
wealth and peace." He now tells the men with him to go on a little
before him and is left alone on the stage.

We now come to Hamlet's last soliloquy, his fourth (unless his
speech over the praying figure of Claudius be considered a soliloquy,
in which case the present soliloquy would be numbered his fifth,
or his speech about the "witching time of night" be so considered,
in which case this would be his sixth). The sight of this army going
out to fight a worthless war for a point of honor serves to stir
Hamlet's shame once more at his own dishonor in having allowed
revenge to be so long delayed: "How all occasions do inform
against me / And spur my dull revenge!" He now asks himself
"what is a man" if his chief value and occupation be "but to sleep
and feed." In line with his recent contemptuous view of man as
engaged solely in eating and being eaten, he answers himself that
such a man is "a beast, no more." Referring now back to the subject of his earlier speech to Rosencrantz and Guildenstern about
the wonderful qualities of man, he reasons that the Creator did not
give man "that capability and godlike reason" so that it would
grow mouldy with disuse.

Realizing that man was given his abilities to accomplish something
more worthy than mere bestial feeding, he now asks himself
whether it was "bestial oblivion" (the forgetfulness of an unaware
animal) or some cowardly "scruple" produced by "thinking too
precisely on th' event" which explains his lack of action on his
revenge. But he finally must conclude: 'I do not know / Why yet
I live to say, 'This thing's to do,' / Sith I have cause, and will,
and strength, and means / To do't."

In comparison with his own shameful lack of action, he now must
witness the behavior of Fortinbras "whose spirit, with divine ambition puffed," exposes his own "mortal and unsure" existence "to
all that fortune, death, and danger dare" for nothing more valuable
than "an eggshell." He concludes from this that to be truly "great"
one must not simply be ready to fight for a sufficient and worthy
cause "But greatly to find quarrel in a straw / When honor's at the
stake." As he had said in the second soliloquy, the man of true
honor is he who has sufficient "gall to make oppression bitter,"
who is willing to fight a duel at the slightest excuse. Once again

he must compare himself with this model of honor, here represented by Fortinbras who is going out to battle to regain his father's lost territories and thus restore the family honor. With both his reason and his natural feelings excited by his father's murder and mother's dishonor, Hamlet can "let all sleep" while, to his "shame," he sees "the imminent death of twenty thousand men" for a merely imagined point of honor. Having shamed himself into renewed commitment to his revenge at a time when such revenge is almost impossible, he concludes strongly: "O, from this time forth, / My thoughts be bloody, or be nothing worth!" With this he leaves to rejoin his companions and the scene ends.

> **COMMENT AND SUMMARY:**   Just before the start of his soliloquy, Hamlet had judged Fortinbras' action as the "imposthume," the abscess or sickness, produced by "much wealth and peace." The claim of the honor code upon his spirit is still strong enough, however, to produce an inward shame at the comparison with his own inaction and to produce this final meditation on the nature of honor. But it is interesting that while he ostensibly convinces himself of the need to pursue honor, he is also undermining the validity of the honor code at its most vulnerable point. He shows that what makes a man of honor superior to a bestial man is simply his willingness to "dare" any danger, and that the reason for this almost suicidal exposing of his life to death is immaterial. Although Hamlet tries to identify the honor code here with religion, calling honor "divine ambition" and claiming that honorable action is a proper use of one's God-given talents, such an identification is highly questionable and is later dropped by Hamlet in favor of a more proper understanding of Divine Providence. Hamlet ends by mourning the unnecessary deaths of twenty thousand men for an imaginary point of honor while himself being convinced by their example to pursue the bloody path to honor. In other words, the very means by which Hamlet renews his commitment to honor serve to undermine his purpose. But this is only a new example of Hamlet's peculiar way of rationalizing himself into momentary self-acceptance. And he will only be left once more with the problem: "I do not know / Why yet I live to say, 'This thing's to do,' / Sith I have cause, and will, and strength, and means / To do't."

This last point refutes those critics who claim that the only reason Hamlet did not accomplish his revenge is that he had no opportunity to do so except in the one case when Claudius was praying, at which time specific scruples prevented him. Here Hamlet states that he has had the "means to do't" and "let all sleep." He also asks himself whether the reason for his delay was, as Coleridge later claimed, that he overintellectualized his problem, an excuse he earlier suggested in the "To be or not to be" soliloquy. But we have seen that, in fact, Hamlet does not think "too precisely on th' event" but uses his reason primarily to rationalize away "all occasions" of action or guilt, and he thus misuses his God-given reason even in the soliloquy in which he condemns such misuse. We are left with the reason that springs first to his mind, "bestial oblivion," the fact that he simply cannot concentrate on the subject of his revenge, but this seems to him so "bestial," something he has just condemned in man, that he immediately goes to the opposite extreme of suggesting that he thinks too much about it, which we have just disproven.

The fact seems to be that Hamlet is guilty of "bestial oblivion," that he then responds to his guilt by producing an intellectualized rationalization, but that this does not ultimately satisfy him and he is left with the mystery of his inaction. Though he had apparently had a change of orientation after the killing of Polonius, we see confirmed here our earlier suspicion at Hamlet's playful hiding of the body, that he is still essentially unchanged in his inability to consciously pursue his revenge against Claudius, and this despite his apparent commitment to this course in the present soliloquy.

ACT IV: SCENE 5

This scene returns us to the castle at Elsinore after a lapse of perhaps a month in time. (This is the first lapse in time since the end of Act I, for all of Act II, Act III, and the first four scenes of Act IV took place in a very crowded twenty-four hour period.) The Queen enters with Horatio and another gentleman. They have been trying to persuade her to see Ophelia, but Gertrude insists: "I will not speak with her." The Gentleman says that Ophelia is very desirous of seeing Gertrude and that her state should be pitied. When Gertrude asks what Ophelia wants with her, the Gentleman only describes her behavior, that "she speaks much of her father" and of the deceit of the world, that she acts and speaks in a disordered wa ywhich observers construe in a lascivious way, though Ophelia's "winks and nods and gestures" seem to support such an interpretation. Horatio urges that " 'Twere good she were spoken with" for she is giving malicious minds unfortunate ideas. Gertrude now relents and tells them to admit Ophelia; the two gentlemen leave and, left alone, Gertrude admits that her "sick soul!" has dreaded to confront any new misfortune because of her already agitated sense of "guilt" (thus showing that Hamlet's efforts to arouse her conscience have had a permanent effect).

Ophelia now enters in a distracted state of insanity. She first asks, "Where is the beauteous majesty of Denmark?" (This is the only objective statement in the play that Gertrude is a beautiful woman and it helps to explain Claudius' love for her, the tender concern of the ghost and, perhaps, even Hamlet's oversensitivity to his mother's sexual activities. Clearly she is a woman fully in her prime.) Though Gertrude addresses her, Ophelia does not seem to know her but starts to sing two snatches of song: the first asks how one is to know her "true-love" from another, and the answer is by his clothes, which are those of a pilgrim; the second snatch of song announces, "He is dead and gone, lady," buried under grass with a stone at his heels. She continues to sing of a burial as Claudius comes in, and he concludes that her insanity was caused by thoughts of her father. Ophelia does not wish to hear of this and, by way of explaining the meaning of her state, sings another song. This is a rowdy ballad about a girl's loss of virginity on St. Valentine's day: her lover opens his chamber door to "Let in the maid, that out a maid / Never departed more"; when she later tells him, "Before you tumbled me, / You promised me to wed," he answers that he would have done so had she "not come to my bed." She now returns to weeping at the thought of her father's death and that "they would lay him i' th' cold ground," reminds them that her "brother shall know of it," and, calling for her coach, departs saying "Good night, ladies." Claudius sends Horatio to look after her and again concludes that her insanity "springs all from her father's death."

COMMENT: Although Claudius rejects the possibility of disappointed love as a cause of Ophelia's insanity, just as he had in the case of Hamlet, it is clear that this contributes as much to her state as the death of her father. Though there is no evidence in the play that Hamlet did seduce Ophelia (despite the opinion of some critics that her St. Valentine's day song does constitute evidence), Hamlet's change from offering honorable love to her to treating her as a discarded whore has evidently convinced her insane mind that she must have yielded to this most guarded against temptation if his rejection of her is to be at all understood. It is clear that she did not understand her responsibility for his change of heart, since she was simply following her father's orders which were designed to protect her from being discarded, and that Hamlet's treatment of her in the "nunnery" and "play" scenes affected her more deeply than was then apparent. Since her "true-love" has betrayed her trust, she no longer knows by what means to recognize him, only knows that there is deceit in the world. That she does not further connect Hamlet with the murder of her father indicates the secrecy with which Claudius has concealed this fact, as he will, himself, mention almost immediately. On the same day as she felt herself so brutally betrayed by her lover, however, she was also faced with the death of her father, a father on whose judgment she had been totally dependent for all her actions and opinions. The effect of this double tragic loss was so overwhelming that it completely destroyed her sanity.

The comparison of her circumstances with those of Hamlet at the beginning of the play should be obvious. Both were faced with the horrible fact of a parent's death at the same time as their trust in one in whose love they had believed was betrayed. Both faced the twin evils of human existence, hypocrisy and death, at the same time and both of their minds were unsettled by this double confrontation with the evils of existence. The fact that Ophelia's reaction duplicates Hamlet's serves to universalize his experience, to give it greater validity as, indeed, the most tragic of human experiences.

But the differing extent of their reactions also serves to illuminate Hamlet's stature. The fact that in similar circumstances Ophelia's mind completely lost its grip on reality reveals Hamlet's greater heroic stature: Hamlet has faced up to a tragic reality which can destroy a lesser spirit and, however unsettled it made him, has maintained a final grip on his sanity. As such Ophelia serves as a "foil" to Hamlet. (A "foil" is the setting of a ring which displays the jewel more advantageously, allowing the light to shine through it and thus make it more brilliant. This image has been taken over by dramatic criticism to refer to a character who serves to illuminate the virtues of the more important central character. It is in this sense that Hamlet, himself, in Act V: Scene 2, says to Laertes as they are about to duel: "I'll be your foil, Laertes. In mine ignorance / Your skill shall, like a star i' th' darkest night, / Stick fiery off indeed.")

Claudius now tells Gertrude that Ophelia's insanity is not their only sorrow: first Ophelia's father was slain; next Gertrude's son was justly exiled; thirdly, the people are confused by Polonius' death since no explanations were given and he was hurriedly and secretly interred; lastly, Laertes has secretly returned from France and, since no true information has been provided, has been filled with rumors of Claudius' own responsibility for Polonius' death. This last fact makes him particularly fearful. At this a noise is heard and a messenger enters. Claudius is so unnerved by this that he

calls for his "Switzers," his hired Swiss guards. The messenger
tells him that he must act to save himself since Laertes at the head
of a riotous rabble has overcome the King's officers. The rabble
mob, having forgotten the ancient hierarchy and customs of society
"cry, 'Choose we! Laertes shall be king!' " At this point another
noise is heard; the King cries "The doors are broke;" and Laertes
with some followers enters demanding the King. Laertes tells his
followers to leave him alone but guard the door, and then he says
to Claudius, "O thou vile king, / Give me my father." The Queen
tries to calm Laertes but he replies: "That drop of blood that's
calm proclaims me bastard." Claudius now asks Laertes the cause
of his rebellion. Gertrude has tried to physically restrain Laertes,
but Claudius tells her to let him go since "There's such divinity
doth hedge a king / That treason can but peep to what it would,
/ Act little of his will." Laertes answers with the question, "Where
is my father?" Claudius answers, "Dead," and Gertrude immediately interjects, "But not by him." Since Claudius now tells him to
demand whatever he wants to know from him, Laertes answers:

> How came he dead? I'll not be juggled with.
> To hell allegiance, vows to the blackest devil,
> Conscience and grace to the profoundest pit!
> I dare damnation. To this point I stand,
> That both worlds I give to negligence,
> Let come what comes, only I'll be revenged
> Most thoroughly for my father.

COMMENT: Laertes' reaction to his father's death stands
in marked contrast to that of Hamlet. Laertes has gathered
a mob together, stormed the palace and is ready both to
revenge himself upon the King and himself take over the
kingdom. How easily Hamlet could have accomplished the
same is shown by Claudius' earlier statement about Hamlet,
"He's loved of the distracted multitude." Since Hamlet is one
of the two royal Danes with a genuine right to the throne
and since he is beloved by the mob, he could have aroused
the mob as easily as Laertes and swiftly swept to this revenge,
regaining the throne through force. But the very fact that
Laertes, without any royal pretensions, could arouse this
same mob to an anarchic overthrowing of ancient custom
shows how illegitimate is such support, how far from justice
and right.

Shakespeare had strongly condemned the mob in his earlier
play, *Julius Caesar,* when he showed how easily it could be
swayed, first by Brutus and then by Antony. In *Troilus and
Cressida,* written a few years after *Hamlet,* he had as strongly

urged the necessity for degree and hierarchy in society as in nature. In a long speech in Act I: Scene 3, Ulysses says: "O, when degree is shak'd, / Which is the ladder to all high designs, / Then enterprise is sick!... / Take but degree away, untune that string, / And hark what discord follows!" In the history plays written just before *Hamlet,* Shakespeare makes the same point. King Henry the Fourth was wrong to have deposed the rightful King Richard the Second even though Richard was not ruling the kingdom well, and it is Henry the Fifth who is the ideal king since he is both a legitimate and good ruler. It is clear, then, that Shakespeare does not approve of regicide and especially disapproves of mob support. Though Laertes has taken the shortest path to success, he has compromised his ends by the means used. That even Laertes is aware of this is indicated by the respect he accords Claudius when Claudius invokes the divine right of kings.

But Laertes further compromises the validity of his revenge by the terms in which he is willing to undertake it. He throws his former allegiance, vows, conscience and grace away, though this means vowing himself "to hell" and to "the blackest devil," and, aware of the religious implications of such revenge, proclaims, "I dare damnation." He is unconcerned about the question of his soul's salvation as long as he can be "revenged most thoroughly for my father."

Such an attitude places Hamlet's predicament in its clearest relief. For Hamlet has always been concerned about this problem. However tempted and even momentarily controlled by the power of hell he may have been, he has never finally been able to commit an act which he felt might damn his soul and has been continually concerned with this question. Though his questioning of the ghost's nature may not have been the primary reason for his delay, it is clearly a problem uppermost in his conscious mind. He is not willing to commit a revenge which would involve his conscious allegiance to hell. It is not only Ophelia, then, but also Laertes who serves as a foil to Hamlet. Laertes shows us that such direct revenge on Hamlet's part would have resulted in both a social crime and spiritual damnation and that Hamlet is the better man for having, unlike Laertes, delayed his revenge.

Claudius now tells Laertes that he will not hinder his revenge but asks whether Laertes means to include in his revenge "both friend and foe." When Laertes answers that he is only opposed to "his enemies" and is willing to learn the true circumstances of his father's death, Claudius says that he will prove to Laertes that he is guiltless of his father's death. At this point Ophelia reenters and Laertes is shocked and grieved to discover his sister's mental state. As Ophelia proceeds to sing of her father's funeral and offer flowers to the various people there, Laertes tells her, "Hadst thou thy wits, and didst persuade revenge, / It could not move thus." Continuing to sing of her father's death as she departs, she leaves a grief-stricken Laertes whom Claudius now turns to comfort. He tells Laertes that he should choose his wisest friends to judge between them as he explains the circumstances of Polonius' death. If they still find him guilty, Claudius is willing to give Laertes his crown and life, but if they find him innocent he says that he will be willing to help Laertes to accomplish his revenge against the truly guilty party. Laertes agrees to this and says that he wishes a full explanation of his father's "obscure funeral" with "no noble rite nor formal ostentation." Claudius says that he shall be satisfied and then "where th' offense is, let the great axe fall." They now all leave to attend to this inquiry.

SUMMARY   This scene accomplishes the following purposes:

1. It shows us further unfortunate effects of Hamlet's killing of Polonius—Ophelia's madness and Laertes' vowed revenge.

2. Both of these unfortunate effects of Hamlet's killing, however, serve ironically as foils to show Hamlet's greater virtue. This is one of the most important dramatic effects in the play. At a point where our respect for Hamlet is at its lowest, due to his inhuman reasons for not killing Claudius, his insane slaughter of Polonius and his contemptuous treatment of his body thereafter, Shakespeare takes him out of both Denmark and our view for a period and shows us situations parallelling Hamlet's. By showing us how similar situations completely destroy Ophelia's sanity and lead Laertes into behavior both criminal and damnable, we are able to more truly judge Hamlet's actions, to see in them not a lack of control but, on the contrary, an extraordinary grip on himself and a grasp of a most agonizing and spiritually dangerous situation. Having shown us Hamlet's flaws with the greatest of detail, Shakespeare is now beginning his rehabilitation as a tragic hero worthy of our admiration.

ACT IV: SCENES 6 AND 7

The sixth scene takes place in another room of the castle immediately following the last. Horatio has been called to this room to meet some sailors who have asked for him. He is given a letter from Hamlet which describes Hamlet's adventures at sea as follows: after they were two days at sea, a pirate ship chased and then came alongside of his ship. Some fighting ensued during which Hamlet alone boarded the pirate ship. (This shows his customary quickness to undertake physical activity when not related to his revenge and refutes the idea of Hamlet as a simply intellectual man.) Immediately the pirate ship got clear of the Danish ship with the result that Hamlet became their prisoner. They have treated him well, however, and Hamlet now means to reward them for the freedom they have given him. He tells Horatio to see that they get to the King with the letters he has sent to Claudius and then that Horatio should come with these "good fellows" to where he is as he has "words to speak in thine ear will make thee dumb." Horatio now leaves with them immediately to go to the King.

The scene now shifts to another room in the castle where the King has been in conference with Laertes. The seventh scene begins with Claudius' conclusion to the inquiry: Laertes must now acquit him since he understands "That he which hath your noble father slain / Pursued my life." Laertes grants him the appearance but asks him why he did not proceed to take justice against the offender who so threatened his own life. Claudius responds that it was "for two special reasons" which might not seem as strong to Laertes as they do to him. The first reason he states as follows:

> The queen his mother
> Lives almost by his looks, and for myself
> My virtue or my plague, be it either which
> She is so conjunctive to my life and soul
> That, as the star moves not but in his sphere
> I could not but by her.

COMMENT: Here Claudius seems to be making a genuine confession of love for Gertrude. It may be that his love is his "plague" since, as we have seen, it did not allow him to repent his murder and so save his soul and is now endangering his life. Or it may be that his love is his "virtue" since it provides the major value and meaning to his life. In any case, she is so necessary to his "life and soul" that even if his love for her destroys both his present life and eternal hope these would both be meaningless without her; he simply cannot live without her. Such a confession may even explain the dreadful murder of his brother. His need to wholly possess his mistress may have become so great that he could no longer live without making her his wife. Such a desperate love, leading as it does to murder, may not be sanctified, but it is certainly more than the simple lust for which Hamlet and

his father's ghost condemn it. And we may even understand
the appeal such a desperate love must have had upon Gertrude. That it is love rather than lust is further shown by
Claudius' tender concern to protect Gertrude from any un-
pleasantness. In Gertrude's unwillingness to see the disturbed
Ophelia, we may see a general characteristic of hers, an unwillingness to be disturbed by anything unpleasant. We can
easily imagine, then, how much the unpleasant necessities of
maintaining a secret adultery must have upset her. Possibly it
was this which made it urgent for Claudius to murder his
brother. Unable to face the possibility of losing her love, this
deed would enable him to return her to the mental peace of
a conventionally married woman. Certainly he took great
pains to conceal the deed from her so that she was able to
enter the marriage without too much moral difficulty. It was
certainly for her sake that he tried to develop good relations
with her son and even now, when her son has clearly indicated his murderous intentions against him, he cannot bear
to alienate her affections by openly condemning her son to
death.

The fact that all his plans for disposing of his vowed enemy
must be done behind her back certainly handicaps him in
dealing effectively with Hamlet. The fact that the death of
Hamlet, even if not ascribed to him, would upset Gertrude is
perhaps responsible for his long hesitation in even taking these
steps. If Hamlet, for known and unknown reasons, has been
hindered from taking effective action against Claudius, there
are also factors which hinder Claudius as much from effectively protecting himself against Hamlet. The first, as indicated by his growing remorse over his murder of his brother,
is his unwillingness to add another sin to his conscience. The
second reason, already mentioned and now to be again repeated, is Hamlet's popularity with the people and his unwillingness to take action against Hamlet which might turn
the people against him. A third unspoken reason may be his
fear of bringing Hamlet before a court where Hamlet might
be able to present his own charges against him. But certainly
the greatest reason is his love for Gertrude.

Claudius now tells Laertes that the second reason he did not
prosecute Hamlet was that he was afraid the "great love" the common people bear for Hamlet would cause his plans to backfire
against himself "and not where I had aimed them." Laertes com-
plains that this does not satisfy his need to revenge the death of
his father and mental breakdown of his sister, but Claudius calms
him with the assurance that he will help him accomplish his
purposes.

At this point a messenger arrives with the letters from Hamlet. Claudius is shocked at this event but he then proceeds to read the following letter to Laertes: "High and mighty, you shall know I am set naked on your kingdom. Tomorrow shall I beg leave to see your kingly eyes; when I shall (first asking your pardon thereunto) recount the occasion of my sudden and more strange return. HAMLET."

> **COMMENT:** Since, as we are soon to learn, Hamlet is well aware of Claudius' plan to have him murdered in England, it is surprising that he should continue to act with so little concern for his own safety. What he does is to warn Claudius of his "naked," that is unarmed and unaccompanied, return into Claudius' power, thus providing Claudius with a new means to plan his destruction. What is more, Hamlet indicates his continuing hatred of Claudius by addressing him rudely as "High and mighty." Hamlet's behavior is in marked contrast to Laertes' mode of re-entry into Denmark, but if it is lacking in treason it is also lacking in even the slightest degree of self-protection, not to speak of any apparent means of attack. Though this may seem foolish on the face of it, it is, as we shall soon see, the product of a new understanding he had gained while on shipboard.

While both Laertes and Claudius are confused by this turn of events, as well they might be, they are quick to see advantage for themselves in it. Laertes says "it warms the very sickness in my heart" that he will be able to return his injury back to Hamlet. Claudius immediately conceives a new plan which will so cleverly dispose of Hamlet that "for his death no wind of blame shall breathe, / But even his mother shall uncharge the practice / And call it accident." Laertes says that he will only be fully satisfied with the plan if he might be its instrument, and Claudius replies that this is in line with his thoughts.

He now tells Laertes about the visit of a Norman two months earlier who astonished the court with his horseback riding. This Norman had known and praised Laertes extravagantly, particularly for his skill in fencing. This had made Hamlet so envious that he had kept wishing for Laertes' sudden return so that he could have a sporting fencing match with him. It is from this fact that Claudius now means to work Hamlet's destruction. Before explaining his idea, however, Claudius asks Laertes how much he loved his father and then, very much like the Player King, reminds him that the passage of time can weaken any purpose and that one should quickly accomplish his will. To his final question as to what he would do to prove himself his father's true son, Laertes replies that he would "cut his throat i' the' church!" And Claudius agrees: "No place indeed should murther sanctuarize; / Revenge should know no bounds." (Here we see most clearly the damnable nature of revenge in its essential opposition with religion. It is ironic that Claudius seconds Laertes' willingness to do that which Hamlet refrained from doing, that is killing a man in prayer, though it is also to Hamlet's discredit that his reason for not then killing Claudius was not Hamlet's reverence for piety. In any case, Laertes' statement underscores his eagerness to "dare damnation" to effect his revenge, and in this he is in marked contrast to Hamlet. Claudius now explains that his plan is to propose a fencing match between Hamlet and Laertes. Since, as just markedly shown by his letter, Hamlet is "remiss, / Most generous, and free from all contriving," he will not examine the foils and Laertes should easily be able to choose a sharply pointed rather than practice foil with which, during the course of the match, he can kill Hamlet. Laertes agrees and, not to be outdone in villainy, adds that he will also dip the tip of his foil in poison so that a mere scratch will prove fatal. Claudius now suggests that if even this should fail there had better be a reserve plan so that their failure would not be apparent. He now suggests that he will prepare a poisoned chalice for Hamlet to drink when he becomes thirsty during the match so that "if he by chance escape your venomed stuck, / Our purpose may hold there."

COMMENT: There is surely something wrong with such a plan, for any death by a sword wound in a practice match in which the foils are supposed to have dull rounded tips could hardly be considered accidental. What is more, if Hamlet were to die after publicly drinking a drink offered by Claudius, this would also cast suspicion on Claudius. Since this plan is so inferior to the "perfect crime" of his first murder, it can only be taken as an indication of Claudius' increasing hysteria in the face of Hamlet's continued dangerous and mocking existence. Laertes is willing to go along with this plan since he feels that any kind of murder would serve to clean the stain off his "honor."

Gertrude now enters with the sorrowful news that Ophelia has drowned and beautifully describes the scene of her death. Ophelia had attempted to hang a wreath of wild flowers on the bough of a willow tree which had grown over a brook and the bough on which she was climbing broke, throwing her into the water below. There she lay for a time, bouyed up by her clothes while she sang snatches of old songs and was incapable of recognizing her danger. At last her drenched garments pulled her down to death.

COMMENT: It might be noted that anyone who could have observed this scene well enough to have reported it to Gertrude would have been criminally negligent in not saving Ophelia from death. Though this problem can be argued away by considering Gertrude's tale as a stage convention for reporting an event which could not be presented on stage, the fact remains that, in the next scene, it is common rumor that Ophelia's death was the result of suicide and this is reflected in the form of her funeral. We are then left with the possibility that Gertrude was told a story which would not upset her, or that she herself elaborated a story which placed Ophelia's death in its least unpleasant light, whether for her own benefit or for Laertes. These possibilities are in line with what we know of Gertrude's character. In view of the general uncertainty about Ophelia's death at the time of the funeral, we can only conclude that her death was unobserved and that Gertrude's version is simply one interpretation after the fact. But the fact that, whether consciously or not, Ophelia's mental condition resulted in her death again serves as a foil to Hamlet's rejection of the temptation of suicide.

Laertes tries to restrain his tears at the recounting of his sister's death but finally is forced to quickly leave the room. Claudius and Gertrude quickly follow to try to comfort him as the fourth act ends.

SUMMARY These last two scenes mark the off-stage return of Hamlet and serve to sharply distinguish him from Claudius and Laertes. While Hamlet is, as Claudius notes, "Most generous, and free from all contriving," Claudius and Laertes busy themselves with treacherously planning his death. The rehabilitation of Hamlet begun in the previous scene is continued in these, even in the face of Ophelia's death.

ACT V: SCENE 1

The scene takes place in a graveyard near the castle at Elsinore on the following day. Two gravediggers, who are to be played by clowns, are discussing the funeral rites of the lady for whom they are preparing a grave. It appears that she is to have a Christian burial though, to their way of thinking, she was clearly a suicide and they resentfully see this as a result of her high position: "And the more pity that great folk should have count'nance in this world to drown or hang themselves more than their even-Christen. Come, my spade. There is no ancient gentlemen but gard'ners, ditchers, and grave-makers. They hold up Adam's profession." Here a more democratic Christian gentility is asserted in the face of the false

aristocratic notion of honor, and the proof of this is in their profession, for their graves serve all and must "last till doomsday."

The chief gravedigger now sends the other for some liquor and,
after he leaves, continues to dig while singing a song of youthful
love: "In youth when I did love, did love, / Methought it was
very sweet." At this point Hamlet and Horatio enter and Hamlet
is surprised that the gravedigger is so lacking in "feeling of his
business, that 'a sings at grave-making." Horatio explains this as
a product of "custom" and Hamlet agrees. The gravedigger now
throws up a skull and Hamlet reflects on the vanity of human
wishes: "How the knave jowls it to the ground, as if 'twere Cain's
jawbone, that did the first murther! This might be the pate of a
politician, which this ass now o'erreaches; one that would circumvent God, might it not? . . . . Or of a courtier, which could say
'Good morrow, sweet lord!' " (Here Hamlet seems to be thinking
of Claudius and such courtiers as Polonius, Rosencrantz and Guildenstern. Claudius has tried to "circumvent God" through a
brother's murder like that of Cain and yet all he shall finally gain
is a death like that which Hamlet has already awarded to Claudius'
courtiers, as we shall soon see. Hamlet's readiness to identify the
skull he sees being rudely thrown about with that of Claudius
shows us that Hamlet has Claudius' coming death very firmly in
mind.) As Hamlet continues to reflect on the generality of death,
however, he becomes upset by it: "Did these bones cost no more
the breeding but to play at loggets with 'em? Mine ache to think
on't." After continuing to reflect on the losses of the grave's occu-
pant, whether lawyer or great landowner, he finally asks the gravedigger whose grave it is. When the gravedigger answers that though
"I do not lie in't, yet it is mine," Hamlet replies in as humorous
a vein, "Thou dost lie in't, to be in't and say it is thine. 'Tis for the
dead, not for the quick; therefore thou liest." (Here we see Hamlet
once more moving quickly from melancholy to punning wit and
still very upset by the fact of death as at the first. But his mood
is more controlled, his melancholy brief, his wit more playful. He
is not a different Hamlet, but he seems to have himself in better
control.) After finally being told that the grave is being prepared
for a woman, Hamlet asks him how long he has been a gravedigger,
and the gravedigger replies that it has been thirty years, that he
began on "that day that our last king Hamlet overcame Fortinbras"
which was also "the very day that young Hamlet was born." (Here
we have our first indication of Hamlet's exact age. Shakespeare has
refrained from informing us that Hamlet was a man rather than a
boy until Hamlet had matured to his full thirty years. As Hamlet is
soon to reach his tragic end, it is important to fully establish his
significance as a grown rather than young man whose actions are
not motivated by youthful disillusionment but mature consideration.

The gravedigger now comes upon the skull of one he knew, Yorick, the king's jester, who had died twenty-three years before. Hamlet takes the skull and says to Horatio: "Alas, poor Yorick! I knew him, Horatio, a fellow of infinite jest, of most excellent fancy. He hath borne me on his back a thousand times. And now how abhorred in my imagination it is! My gorge rises at it. Here hung those lips that I have kissed I know not how oft. Where be your gibes now?" (In his disturbance over Yorick's death, Hamlet may also begin to fear his own since he is also "a fellow of infinite jest, of most excellent fancy." Indeed, the gravedigger's mention of Hamlet's age reminds him that he has already lived a full generation, and he is soon to leap into this very grave dug by one who has been preparing graves since the day Hamlet was born. If death is waiting for Claudius, it may also be waiting for him.) When Hamlet now begins to wonder whether one's imagination can "trace the noble dust of Alexander till 'a find it stopping a bunghole," Horatio sanely advises him that " 'Twere to consider too curiously, to consider so." Hamlet, however, continues to elaborate this subject, just as he had after Polonius' death, until he is interrupted by the approach of a funeral party led by the King. He notes that the "maimed rites" indicate the funeral of a suicide and he decides to withdraw with Horatio to observe the event unseen.

After the entrance of the King, Queen, Laertes, a Doctor of Divinity, and other lords following the corpse, Laertes suddenly cries out: "What ceremony else?" The Doctor of Divinity explains that since "her death was doubtful," they have enlarged her funeral rites as much as they could and are at least burying her with prayers in sanctified ground rather than throwing rocks on her unsanctified grave. The disgusted Laertes is forced to agree to the funeral but tells the Doctor, "A minist'ring angel shall my sister be / When thou liest howling." At this the shocked Hamlet says, "What, the fair Ophelia?" Gertrude now scatters flowers on Ophelia's grave with the sad mother's reflection: "I hope thou shouldst have been my Hamlet's wife. / I thought thy bride-bed to have decked, sweet maid, / And not have strewed thy grave." But her mention of Hamlet enrages Laertes with the remembrance of Hamlet's guilt for all his family's woes, and he exclaims: "O, treble woe / Fall ten times treble on that cursed head / Whose wicked deed thy most ingenious sense / Deprived thee of!" At the thought of her fate he longs to embrace her once more and, leaping into the grave, calls upon the gravediggers to bury him with her under such a mountain that it "o'ertop old Pelion" or Olympus itself. (This refers to the mythical war in which the Titans attempted to pile the mountain Ossa upon the mountain Pelion in order to reach the heaven of the Olympian gods.)

At this point Hamlet (aroused, as he later says, "into a tow'ring

passion" by the ostentatious display of Laertes' grief and also perhaps by his sense of guilt at Laertes' accusation of his responsibility
- Ophelia's death) comes forward, questions Laertes' right to such
grief when he, "Hamlet the Dane" is there, and leaps into the grave
after Laertes. Laertes begins to fight with him, saying, "The devil
take thy soul!" But Hamlet objects to this prayer and his reply
further indicates his self-awareness of his dangerous tendency to
rashness: "Thou pray'st not well. / I prithee take thy fingers from
my throat, / For though I am not splenitive and rash, / Yet have I
in me something dangerous, / Which let they wisdom fear." Though
he has leaped belligerently into the grave, he tries to control himself
from fighting with Laertes and especially right there in Ophelia's
grave. After they have parted and leave the grave, however, Hamlet
says that he is willing to fight Laertes to the death on the subject
of his love for Ophelia. Though Laertes holds him guilty of her
death, he proclaims: "I loved Ophelia. Forty thousand brothers /
Could not with all their quantity of love / Make up my sum." Hamlet is willing to match any attempt on Laertes' part to prove his
love for Ophelia. If Laertes wishes "to outface me with leaping in
her grave," so will he and will call down as much earth to cover
them as will "make Ossa like a wart!" He concludes his unseem-
ingly harangue with the words "I'll rant as well as thou," at which
point his mother explains to Laertes that "this is mere madness."
She continues her explanation by saying that for "a while the fit
will work on him" and then, "as patient as the female dove," he
will silently "sit drooping." Upon hearing his mother's words, he
does calm himself sufficiently to ask Laertes: "What is the reason
that you use me thus? / I loved you ever." With no apparent
awareness of his responsibility for the deaths of Laertes' father
and sister and for his present disruption of Ophelia's funeral, he
self-righteously concludes: "But it is no matter. / Let Hercules himself do what he may, / The cat will mew, and dog will have his
day." Believing that no amount of heroic endeavor would keep a
low animal like Laertes from making noises at him, he abruptly
turns from them and leaves.

> **COMMENT:** Hamlet's behavior at Ophelia's funeral calls
> for some discussion. Though his tender regard for her is
> momentarily revived at the moment he becomes aware of her
> death, the time when he could approach love simply is as far
> behind him now as it is for the gravedigger whom he had
> just heard singing, "In youth when I did love, did love, /
> Methought it was very sweet." This memory of former love
> immediately becomes mingled with a sense of guilt when
> Laertes accuses him unseen of responsibility for her death.
> Though Hamlet has not been told the reasons for Ophelia's
> death and so might not immediately guess his responsibility
> for her apparent suicide, he tries to suppress the sense of

guilt occasioned by Laertes' words by clutching that memory of former feeling and so heightening it that he can prove his love superior to that anyone else can feel (just as, in his very first long speech in the play, he had tried to prove his integrity to be superior to that of all others at the court).

This seems to be the explanation of Hamlet's challenging leap into the grave and showy proclamation of love for Ophelia as the excuse for his behavior. Any true love for her would hardly express itself in such emotionally exaggerated terms, exaggeration which had angered him when similarly expressed by Laertes. But as he is angered by Laertes' loud show of grief even as it stings his conscience, he tries to evade his guilt by affirming the continuity of his deep love for Ophelia and the superiority of his love to that of Laertes. He challenges Laertes to this test of love quite blinded as to Laertes' just grounds for hating him. At the funeral, he had said to Horatio: "That is Laertes, a very noble youth." Aware only of his own feelings, first for Ophelia, now for Laertes, he cannot understand why Laertes should be treating him so rudely: "What is the reason that you use me thus? / I loved you ever." And when Laertes refuses to condone Hamlet's present and past behavior, Hamlet's self-righteous involvement with his own feelings reaches a dreadful climax in the contemptuous insults he hurls at Laertes in apparent requital for his own wrongs.

Hamlet still reveals a complete lack of sympathy for anyone whom he believes to be wronging him. As he acted this way with Polonius, Ophelia and, as we shall soon see, Rosencrantz and Guildenstern, so does he here with Laertes. This whole scene at the funeral marks, indeed, one of Hamlet's lowest moral points. We see him essentially unchanged from the man who belittled and then murdered Polonius and could then still mock his corpse. But there is this slight development of self-awareness and control that he is now aware that there is something in him which can make him dangerously rash and, though he has acted rashly enough in leaping into the grave and making such an unseemly scene, he does exert his utmost power to control himself from rashly murdering Laertes.

Claudius tells Horatio to follow Hamlet and then tells Laertes to keep his patience in the memory of the previous night's conference and in the assurance that very soon "this grave shall have a living monument," that is, the life of Hamlet. Upon this note of discord between Hamlet and Laertes, the scene ends.

SUMMARY   This scene has the following important aspects:

1. The gravediggers' joking about death provides some comic relief just before the final scene of multiple death at the same time that it prepares us thematically for this outcome.

2. In Hamlet's easy familiarity with the gravediggers, as earlier with the players and pirates and with his less well-born college friends, we see the true gentility of one who, being "to the manner born," is able to forget his special aristocratic privileges and become "even-Christen" with all men of good will. In this he stands in immediate contrast with Laertes, who always stands upon "ceremony."

3. In addition to this democratic quality, we are shown a variety of Hamlet's moods by which we may gauge the extent of his development before the final tragic scene. We see Hamlet still considering "too curiously" the common horror of death and still reacting to such horror with his characteristic alternation of melancholy and wit. Though he seems to be in firmer control of himself, this control is still imperfect and almost completely breaks down at the sight of Ophelia's grave and Laertes' showy grief. And though he is so sensitive to the horrors of existence, he can still show himself as completely insensitive to the feelings and rights of others if he believes himself to be wronged by them. He is still highly unstable, able to go at any moment into an irrational state in which he is capable of rash cruelty, but he is more aware of this now and better able to control himself than formerly.

4. At the moment when Hamlet offers to duel with Laertes and then when he asks him his grievance, Laertes has the opportunity to explain himself honestly to Hamlet and then either accept their mutual love for Ophelia as reason for their reconciliation or attempt to revenge his father's death in an honorable duel to the death. Laertes, however, is so angered by the blind self-righteousness of this murderer of his family that he cannot be open with him and continues to nurse his secretive and ignoble revenge. Claudius is easily able to use Hamlet's irrational behavior as a means of strengthening Laertes' allegiance to himself and insuring the speedy enactment of their plan.

ACT V: SCENE 2

The final scene takes place in a major hall of the castle at Elsinore soon after the funeral. Hamlet enters in the act of explaining his recent behavior to Horatio. He immediately comes to the important events on shipboard which, in his letter to Horatio, he had said would make Horatio "dumb." In all of his soliloquies, he precedes his discussion of events with generalizations he has drawn from them. What he did on shipboard was rash and, in what is probably the most significant speech in the play, he now explains the culminating insight of his experience:

> And praised be rashness for it—let us know,
> Our indiscretion sometime serves us well
> When our deep plots do pall, and that should learn us
> There's a divinity that shapes our ends,
> Rough-hew them how we will—

Shakespeare has Horatio underscore the significance of these statements by saying, "That is most certain."

COMMENT: What Hamlet has learned is that man cannot carve out his own destiny but that this is ultimately shaped by Providence. Such an idea is not new to him or to the play, for he had earlier expressed it in the following lines given to the Player King: "Our wills and fates do so contrary run / That our devices still are overthrown; / Our thoughts are ours, their ends none of our own." The "devices" and "deep plots" by which man attempts to shape his fate cannot achieve final success since man is and must recognize that he is dependent upon Divine Providence. Hamlet's experiences now cause him to accept this idea with full conviction. Human ends can only be realized when they express the will of heaven and this, in turn, requires man to make himself into an agent for the divine will, acting only when seized by divine inspiration.

Such a person moves from the simple religion based upon obedience to the written law of God to the more difficult and often tragic religion of prophet and saint which is based upon obedience to the personally received commandments of God, commandments which often involve violations of the written law. The best example of this, as the great nineteenth century Danish theologian Søren Kierkegaard pointed out in *Fear and Trembling,* is Abraham's willingness to obey the divine commandment to sacrifice his son Isaac to God, even though this involves the violation of the moral written commandment against murder. Such obedience may lead to martyrdom but, as the prophet Isaiah has explained of the nature of divine election, the Lord says "I have chosen thee in the furnace of affliction." The tragic reality of religion is that God often sacrifices his best and most beloved servants to achieve His will for the good of the whole. This is, in fact, the essence of the Christian mystery. And this is also Shakespeare's great understanding of reality.

For Shakespeare the essential moral distinction between men is not simply between those who do good and those who do evil, but between those who recognize their dependence upon the divine will and are willing to follow it to whatever end it demands and those who reject the idea of their dependence upon God and, in a modern secular spirit, believe that they alone must bear the responsibility for shaping their destiny. Thus, in *Julius Caesar,* the villain Cassius says to Brutus: "The fault, dear Brutus, is not in our stars, / But in ourselves, that we are underlings." And in *King Lear* the villain Edmund says: "This is the excellent foppery of the world, that, when we are sick in fortune, often the surfeit of our own behavior, we make guilty of our disasters the sun, the moon, and the stars; as if we were villains on necessity; fools by heavenly compulsion; knaves, thieves, and treachers by spherical predominance; drunkards, liars, and adulterers by an enforc'd obedience of planetary influence; and all that we are evil in, by a divine thrusting on." Similarly the villain Macbeth, in the tragedy which bears his name, though saying "If chance will have me King, why, chance may crown me, / Without my stir," does not leave his foretold destiny to "chance" but tries to shape his ends directly.

Shakespeare's villains, then, begin their course with an attitude which sounds very sensible to modern ears, that if there is such a thing as divinity it is quite irrelevant to human actions and that if man is to achieve anything in this world he can only do so through his own efforts. But such an attitude places man alone in the universe and thereby causes man to see himself as its center. This cosmic loneliness joined to a necessary egocentricity then leads to man's sense of alienation from his own community. What he desires is alone important. There is nothing, therefore, which can hinder him from attempting to achieve his desires at whatever the cost to others. At this point he becomes capable of any villainy. This is the genesis of Shakespeare's villains and, though less articulated by Claudius, also explains his behavior.

Claudius has made himself the god of his universe. This he indicates throughout the play by his celebration of his own power with trumpets, drums and cannons: "But the great cannon to the clouds shall tell, / And the king's rouse the heaven shall bruit again, / Respeaking earthly thunder." If he desires his brother's crown and wife, he acts to take them; if he must preserve his gains through the murder of Hamlet, he is ever ready to use "deep plots" to shape events to his own ends.

In opposition to this, Hamlet has been ever engaged in trying to fathom the divine will, has come to recognize his dependence upon it, the futility of all humanly conceived plots, and the primary necessity of only acting, in Edmund's words, with "a divine thrusting on." It is this, as we shall soon see, which motivates all of Hamlet's actions after his return to Denmark and which, in spite of all the murders he accomplishes, far more than those of the villain Claudius, makes him fit to be Shakespeare's tragic hero.

Hamlet now explains that one night on shipboard he felt so extremely restless that he "rashly" left his cabin, found his way in the dark to the cabin of Rosencrantz and Guildenstern, discovered their package of letters, and returned to his own cabin. Once there, he was "so bold" as to "unseal / Their grand commission; where I found, Horatio— / Ah, royal knavery!—an exact command" that without any loss of time, "No, not to stay the grinding of the axe, / My head should be struck off." Hamlet gives this important piece of concrete evidence against Claudius into the care of a shocked Horatio. He then continues his story. Surrounded as he was "with villainies," he again acted upon impulse without any prior planning of this course of action: "Or I could make a prologue to my brains, / They had begun the play." Although he had earlier considered fine penmanship the mark of a lower mind and had tried to forget his early training in fine handwriting, this training now served him well for it enabled him to write a formal state document. He immediately "devised a new commission, wrote it fair," and demanded of the English King that without any debating of this order "He should the bearers put to sudden death, / Not shriving time allowed."

When Horatio asks him how he was able to seal this forged commission, Hamlet replies, "Why, even in that was heaven ordinant. / I had my father's signet in my purse." That he was able with this model of the Danish seal to make a perfect forgery Hamlet sees as a sign of the shaping hand of heaven in these events. And further, the whole exploit by which he discovered Claudius' villainous designs against himself, was able to convert this plan so that it would lead to the destruction of Claudius' accomplices, and then return the forged commission so that the change was never known, finally led him to his grand conclusion that "There's a divinity that shapes our ends, / Rough-hew them how we will."

Horatio now notes in what must be a faintly disapproving tone, "So Guildenstern and Rosencrantz go to't." But Hamlet strongly justifies his actions with words:

Why, man, they did make love to this employment.
They are not near my conscience; their defeat
Does by their own insinuation grow.
'Tis dangerous when the baser nature comes
Between the pass and fell incensed points
Of mighty opposites.

Horatio's next comment, "Why, what a king is this!" enables Hamlet to come to the real issue on his conscience, the question of
regicide:

Does it not, think thee, stand me now upon—
He that hath killed my king, and whored my mother,
Popped in between th' election and my hopes,
Thrown out his angle for my proper life,
And with such coz'nage—is't not perfect conscience
To quit him with this arm? And is't not to be damned
To let this canker of our nature come
In further evil?

COMMENT: We see from this last speech that Hamlet's
conscience had not earlier been perfectly convinced of the
rightness of killing a king. By waiting until this time, however,
and forcing Claudius to show his hand, he now has solid
ground for proceeding to enact not simply a possibly damnable personal revenge, but clear justice. The initial strong
reason for action, Claudius' regicide against Hamlet's father,
followed by the supporting though less mortal indictments
against Claudius of incestuous adultery with his mother and
of winning the election to the throne which Hamlet had hoped
would come to him, has been superceded by Claudius' attack
upon his own life. He is not now going to revenge his father's
murder on the basis of spectral evidence from an unknown
supernatural source, a course of premeditated action which
might be damnable. He is acting in self protection to openly
rid Denmark of a king who has gained and would keep his
throne through recourse to repeated, secretive murders of
which Hamlet has concrete evidence. Not to act in this clear
case of justice would now be as damnable as personal revenge
on behalf of family honor might earlier have been. In this new
bid for personal justice, his father's murder is but the first
item in a long list of Claudius' injuries to him which has
culminated in Claudius' hidden attempt to have him murdered.

But while it is commendable for Hamlet's conscience to be
so concerned to establish the justice of his actions against
Claudius, it is all the more surprisng that his own planned

murders of Rosencrantz and Guildenstern "are not near my conscience." Though his present attitude towards them is less offensive than was his attitude towards Polonius immediately after his murder of him, his justification is the same: "Take thy fortune. / Thou find'st to be too busy is some danger." Once Rosencrantz and Guildenstern have forfeited his trust by hesitating a single moment before confessing that they were sent for, Hamlet has no further use for them. Though they were childhood and college friends of his, he immediately sets them down as no more than corrupt accomplices of a vile king, and that very evening, in his mother's room, is already anticipating his destruction of them.

If it is true that they were carrying sealed orders for his murder, there is no evidence that they had any knowledge of the contents of this commission. Nor does their compliance with Claudius' wishes constitute definite proof of their baseness. They were sent for by their King, a King who had proved himself a good ruler, concerned for his people's welfare, and who seemed to be showing a benevolent concern for Hamlet's health in thus sending for them in the expressed hope that they might help him to understand and thereby cure Hamlet's disorder. During their single day at court, Hamlet's wild behavior after the performance of the play, his murder of Polonius and subsequent display of irrational playfulness could only have convinced them that Hamlet was dangerously mad and that Claudius was taking the most lenient course open to a king forced to protect himself. Though they ally themselves so fully with the King's purposes after the murder of Polonius as to appear high-handed with Hamlet, there is no other way for them to act since Hamlet has grown increasingly belligerent toward them during the course of the day. Moreover, their horror at the possibility of regicide is no different from what Hamlet, himself, would have felt in their place. Indeed, even in his position of revenger, Hamlet's conscience was apparently so disturbed by the complication of regicide involved in his revenge that he did not feel perfectly free to proceed until his own life was placed in danger. Finally, the very extenuation of self-defense, which Hamlet provides for his own coming murder of Claudius, is equally applicable to Claudius' present designs against Hamlet. How much more, then, does Claudius seem to be justified in the simple exiling of Hamlet, which is all that Rosencrantz and Guildenstern would most probably have been told of Claudius' designs.

It would seem, then, that Hamlet is being unfair in condemning Rosencrantz and Guildenstern to death for their apparently innocent obedience to their King. But, as we have seen that Hamlet wishes his revenge to extend beyond Claudius' mortal life, so does he feel it should extend to all the accomplices of his illegitimate reign, and these too he feels should be withheld from going to heaven just as his father was by Claudius' refusal to allow him "shriving time." This explicit addition to Claudius' own order for hasty death shows us that Hamlet's moral condition is still not perfect. He has acted with excessive severity towards Rosencrantz and Guildenstern and still feels no guilt for his action.

Even as Hamlet reaches his most profound and objective justification for his coming murder of Claudius, we see that he already stands far more guilty of wanton death than Claudius. Where Claudius is guilty of regicide and of planning the murder of the heir apparent, Hamlet is guilty of the direct deaths of Polonius, Rosencrantz and Guildenstern and the indirect death of Ophelia. Though Claudius' murders may make up in quality what they lack in quantity, Hamlet has certainly compromised the purity of his intentions by the murderous course he has travelled toward his end, a course for which universal justice will exact its punishment regardless of the fact that it is on the life of its own "scourge and minister."

Horatio now stresses the practical need of speedy action since Claudius will undoubtedly be soon informed of the result of his mission to England. Hamlet blandly agrees: "It will be short; the interim is mine, / And a man's life no more than to say 'one.' "

COMMENT: Hamlet feels quite confident, both of the ease with which he can murder Claudius now that his conscience is perfectly clear, and that he will accomplish this task in the interim before the arrival of the ambassador from England. From Hamlet's behavior during this interim, however, it is also clear that he has made no plan as to how or when he will kill Claudius. He has acted and continues to act in a way which is almost foolhardy in being so extremely "free from all contriving." First he sends word to Claudius that he is returning without any effort at self-protection. Next he virtually ignores Claudius at the funeral which he so angrily disrupts. Finally, he spends his remaining free time engaged, as we shall soon see, in a fencing match with Laertes. From this it should be evident that Hamlet, in accordance with his new understanding of the divine control over human events, has placed his entire reliance upon Providence, confident that the "divinity that shapes our ends" will arrange the circumstances necessary for his action and do this better than he could himself.

But now that his own revenge seems so close to accomplishment,
he suddenly becomes aware of Laertes' just grievance against himself and feels "very sorry" that "to Laertes I forgot myself." Although he excuses his treatment of Laertes on the grounds that
"the bravery [ostentation] of his grief did put me / Into a tow'ring
passion," he hopes to be able to gain Laertes' forgiveness and vows,
"I'll court his favors."

At this providential moment of Hamlet's concern to regain Laertes'
goodwill, the courtier Osric enters with a message of welcome from
Claudius. Turning aside to Horatio and finding that he does not
know "this waterfly," Hamlet tells Horatio that he is the better for
not knowing such an ostentatious, land wealthy fool, and it is
characteristic of Claudius that, though "a beast be lord of beasts,"
he allows him to eat at his own "mess." Osric doffs his hat before
Hamlet as he is about to deliver his message, but Hamlet demo-
cratically tells him to return his hat to his head. When Osric refuses
on the grounds that "it is very hot," Hamlet begins to make fun of
him as he earlier had with Polonius, insisting first that it is cold and
then hot, Osric agreeing to everything Hamlet says, until Hamlet
finally prevails on Osric to wear his hat. Ostric now tries to get to
the point of his coming, the "great wager" the King has placed on
Hamlet's head. When he begins to extol Laertes' merits in the most
ridiculously affected manner, however, Hamlet cannot restrain himself from imitating Osric's absurd manner of speech. But Osric is
too foolishly vain of his own accomplishments to realize that Hamlet is making fun of him and replies: "Your lordship speaks most
infallibly of him." Hamlet continues his marvelous caricature of
Osric, to the delight of Horatio, until he finally gets the bewildered
Osric to come to the point of the wager. Regaining his speech with
all its affection, Osric now explains that Claudius has wagered six
Barbary horses against six French rapiers and poniards that in a
fencing match between Hamlet and Laertes, of a dozen passes,
Laertes would not exceed Hamlet by three hits. The odds are laid
twelve to nine in Hamlet's favor. He now wishes to know whether
Hamlet is willing for this match to come "to immediate trial," and
Hamlet answers that he is willing to have the foils brought immediately to this very hall and to begin the match, that Osric can deliver
this message "after what flourish your nature will." After Osric
leaves, Hamlet and Horatio continue to comment on the comic
absurdity of courtiers like Osric until another lord enters from
Claudius to know whether Hamlet still wishes to play immediately
with Laertes or would "take longer time." As Hamlet says that he
is ready if the King so wishes, the lord informs him tnat the King,
Queen and court are coming to the match and that the Queen
desires Hamlet to greet Laertes in a gentlemanly fashion before they
start to play. Hamlet says that he will follow this instruction and
the lord leaves.

When they are once more alone, Horatio suggests that Hamlet will "lose this wager," but Hamlet disagrees as he has been "in continual practice" since Laertes went to France and should be able to "win at the odds." Nonetheless, he feels a premonition of danger in his heart, though he rejects such "foolery." Horatio advises Hamlet to obey his intuitions and says that he will delay the match on the grounds that Hamlet is not well. But Hamlet replies:

> Not a whit, we defy augury. There is special providence in the fall of a sparrow. If it be now, 'tis not to come; if it be not to come, it will be now; if it be not now, yet it will come. The readiness is all. Since no man of aught he leaves knows, what is't to leave betimes? Let be.

COMMENT: This speech is one of Hamlet's most important utterances. Here we see Hamlet's most complete statement of his belief in the providential nature of all events. As every event down to "the fall of a sparrow" has been determined by the special concern of Providence, one will die whenever and only whenever it has been appointed. Moreover, no man "knows" anything of what he has left behind once he is dead. (It is unclear here whether Hamlet is denying the existence of an afterlife, the survival of personal consciousness or merely the survival of a spirit's earthly memory. Since even the last two would seem to contradict the evidence provided by the ghost, assuming him to be "honest," it is possible that Hamlet may be here defining the nature of spiritual salvation, and that the process of Purgatory is to purge the spirit of its disquieting personal memories and egocentricity so that it can achieve this final salvation.) The fact of death, therefore, need provide no concern for man.

The important thing is to achieve a state of "readiness." In Shakespeare's later development of this idea in *King Lear,* the virtuous Edgar says to his despairing father Gloucester: "What, in ill thoughts again? Men must endure / Their going hence, even as their coming hither; / Ripeness is all. Come on." What is important is not the length of life but its quality. Life is given to a man so that he may develop to his full "ripeness," a state which is reached when he has developed sufficient insight into his true position in the cosmic order to give him the proper "readiness" to endure both life and death. This is the highest moral development of which man is capable and it also serves to distinguish between Shakespeare's heroes and villains. Where Shakespeare's heroes achieve this "readiness," this "ripeness" which is "all," before death, his villains meet "untimely" deaths for which they are spiritually unprepared.

The proof that Hamlet has achieved this "readiness" is given in the last words of this speech, "Let be." This is the one attitude of which Hamlet was earlier incapable. When faced with the horror of death and infidelity, his spirit refused to let it be. Rather than accept the evils of existence, he felt impelled to either sucide or revenge, though these impulses showed "a will most incorrect to heaven." Though this consciousness of evil warped his sensitive nature to the point that he felt "I must be cruel only to be kind" and acted as such, his spirit also began to develop a new healing consciousness of the providential nature of reality. The "Everlasting" was no longer viewed as the harsh, damning lawgiver whose creation thus became a sterile farce, but as a sanctifying Providence, inspiring man with a new liberation of spirit to do and affirm the work of the "Divinity." This is very much the central Christian message preached by St. Paul in his epistles to the Galatians, Corinthians, Romans and Ephesians. Hamlet has now transcended his earlier despair through an affirmation of spirit which reveals his true spiritual heroism.

The King and court now arrive to the accompaniment of trumpets and drums. While the hall is being prepared for the fencing match, Claudius places Laertes' hand into Hamlet's in an apparent bid for their reconciliation. Hamlet begins in the most cordial terms by saying: "Give my your pardon, sir. I have done you wrong, / But pardon't, as you are a gentleman." As Gertrude had done twice before, he now attempts to excuse his behavior on the grounds of madness, a madness which, as he also said over the corpse of Polonius, punishes him as much as his victims: "His madness is poor Hamlet's enemy." If Hamlet "when he's not himself does wrong Laertes," he can at least offer in his own defense: "Let my disclaiming from a purposed evil / Free me so far in your most generous thoughts / That I have shot my arrow o'er the house / And hurt my brother."

COMMENT: Hamlet's defense of unpremeditated murder, caused by temporary insanity, for which his mother is witness, would stand up in our own courts and lead to his acquittal. What is more, it is also true that he has only hurt himself through this unpremeditated act by adversely affecting those he loved (Ophelia and Laertes), and by causing Claudius and Laertes to seek his own life. And what is objectively true in the case of his killing of Polonius also seems to him subjectively true in the case of Rosencrantz and Guildenstern. Here we may be less convinced by his argument, though he carefully stresses to Horatio the rash spontaneity with which he acted against them. He may be guilty of more killing than Claudius, but Claudius' past and future murders of father and son would legally be considered first degree murders, while Hamlet's lack of "purposed evil" might reduce the charges against him to manslaughter or acquittal. In terms of our own legal structure, as well as Shakespeare's moral system, Hamlet's actions, while certainly not safe to society, do finally appear less criminal than Claudius' actions and so should free him in our "most generous thoughts."

Laertes admits that he is "satisfied in nature" though it is this which should stir him most to his revenge, but he is not willing to make a formal reconciliation with Hamlet until "some elder masters of known honor" can show him by precedents that his honor will not be stained by such a peace. Until that time, however, he says that he will "not wrong" Hamlet's offering of love. Hamlet embraces Laertes' reply and is ready to begin "this brother's wager." They call for the foils and, making a pun on the word "foil," Hamlet generously tells Laertes, "I'll be your foil," his own poor performance making Laertes' skill shine the more brightly. As they go to choose the foils, Hamlet seems to convince Laertes that he does not "mock" him. Hamlet is satisfied with the foil he chooses but Laertes is not and goes to choose another foil while Claudius explains to Hamlet once more the terms of the wager. As they prepare to play, Hamlet asks whether the foils are all alike, that is, have dulled ends, and Osric replies, "Ay, my good lord."

COMMENT: In Laertes' reply to Hamlet's apology, we see again his primary concern with "ceremony" and "terms of honor" rather than with the deeper emotional reality of a situation. Though Hamlet seems to have genuinely touched Laertes and perhaps confused his purposes, it does not prevent Laertes from choosing the fatally sharp and poisoned sword while Claudius connives to distract Hamlet's attention. In his concern for the outward appearances of honor, then, Laertes is really dishonoring himself as he goes against his sworn word not to "wrong" Hamlet's love. Osric's assurance to Hamlet about the similarity of the foils suggests that he is also in on the plot. But it is possible that the foils may have been grouped for him by Claudius or Laertes without his knowledge of the sharpened foil.

Claudius now calls for wine to be placed on a table and says that if Hamlet hits Laertes in the first three exchanges "the king shall drink to Hamlet's better breath." He will then drop a rich "union" or pearl into the cup for Hamlet while "the kettle to the trumpet speak, / The trumpet to the cannoneer without, / The cannons to the heaven, the heaven to earth." They begin to play and on the first exchange Hamlet scores, as Osric says, "A hit, a very palpable hit." The drum, trumpets and cannon sound and the King stops the play to drink to Hamlet, drop the pearl into the cup and offer the ceremonial cup to im.

> **COMMENT:** The pearl which Claudius drops in the cup after he drinks from it is apparently the means by which the drink is poisoned. It is interesting that he accompanies this attempt to shape his destiny by the thunderous sounds of his self-deification which are to resound from "heaven to earth." But we may wonder at Claudius' haste to poison Hamlet. This can only be explained by his loss of faith in Laertes' willingness or ability to fulfill his part of their agreement. Perhaps Claudius believed Laertes' promise of fair play to Hamlet; perhaps he senses in Laertes' performance a hesitance to play up to his full ability. Certainly, Laertes' fencing is so poor that, by the third exchange, even Hamlet taunts him with this. At any rate, Claudius turns almost immediately to what was supposed to be left as a last resort.

Hamlet, however, unceremoniously refuses to join Claudius in a toast and asks that the cup be set by awhile until he finishes the next bout. He calls for the beginning of the second bout and immediately makes "another hit," as Laertes confesses.

Claudius now tells Gertrude "our son shall win." In apparent delight over his son's good performance, she goes to wipe Hamlet's brow with her handkerchief. As this brings her close to the table near the fencers on which the cup has been placed, she picks up the cup and tells Hamlet that she too is going to toast his fortune. To this action Hamlet exclaims "Good madam!" but Claudius calls out to her imperiously, "Gertrude, do not drink." She insists, however, "I will, my lord; I pray you pardon me." In silent agony, Claudius reflects: "It is the poisoned cup; it is too late." Hamlet still does not wish to interrupt his fencing and says to her, "I dare not drink yet, madam—by and by." She then goes to wipe his face once more before he starts to play again.

> **COMMENT:** It has been suggested that Gertrude acts in a spirit of motherly self-sacrifice because she suspects the cup's poisoned contents and that Hamlet's exclamation reflects his own suspicions. But such suspicions would hardly account for their subsequent actions, Hamlet's insistence upon continuing his match with Laertes and Gertrude's coming forth to wipe his brow once more. It seems more likely, therefore, that Gertrude is acting with fatal consistency to her character. We have seen that Gertrude tends to withdraw from any unpleasant truth and to delude herself that all is or, at any rate, will be well. She knows that Laertes means to revenge his

father's murder and probably suspects that Claudius has explained Hamlet's responsibility for Polonius' death to him. Her fears were then so aggravated by Hamlet's insulting behavior to Laertes at Ophelia's funeral that she sent special word to Hamlet to apologize to Laertes and try to be reconciled to him. In an unusually tense state, she was delighted by Hamlet's gentlemanly behavior towards Laertes and their apparent reconciliation. Not only that, but Hamlet has been willing to fight as Claudius' champion which seems to promise their reconciliation as well. And Hamlet's reasonable and sportsmanlike behavior seems also to promise her that Hamlet has finally been cured of his dreadful madness. If all this were true, then her growing fears of a great catastrophe might all be forgotten and all might yet be well. Since this is what she most fervently wishes to believe, she accomplishes the miracle of self-delusion once more and comes to believe it so fully that she must actively join into this happy occasion and show her son how happy he has made her. Her inability to face any unpleasant truth is her tragic flaw and it now destroys her. At this fateful moment Claudius might yet have prevented her death by confessing to the poison. But since he is unable to protect her without giving himself away, he chooses his own survival and his throne over his love and can only look on in shocked horror at the ironic twisting of destiny which brings the poison to her lips instead of to Hamlet's as he had designed it. With all this, he too deludes himself into thinking that he can still shape his ends.

As the third round is about to start, Laertes tells Claudius that he will hit Hamlet in this bout. Claudius replies that he doubts it and Laertes admits to himself, "And yet it is almost against my conscience." Hamlet now playfully taunts Laertes about his poor performance, "You but daily," to which Laertes responds, "Say you so? Come on." Playing now to his best ability, Laertes can only bring Hamlet to a draw by the end of the bout. Enraged, he lunges at Hamlet after the close of the round—"Have at you now!"—and manages to wound Hamlet. When Hamlet realizes by his wound that Laertes has been fencing with an illegally sharp sword, he returns the attack with such fury that he gains control of the poisoned weapon in exchange for his own with which he seriously wounds Laertes.

COMMENT: As Gertrude was destroyed by her tragic flaw, so is Laertes by his tragic flaw of false pride and honor. As Laertes' better instincts begin to disturb his conscience, there is a moment when he might have dropped his dishonorable vindictive design against Hamlet in that true spirit of reconciliation which he had pledged but violated. But at this crucial moment, Hamlet makes the fatal mistake of playfully taunting Laertes. This immediately touches Laertes' ever sensitive pride about outward appearances. Playing now as best he can, he feels so dishonored by his inability to defeat Hamlet that he completely dishonors himself by attacking Hamlet after the close of the bout. Jealousy, pride and a false sense of honor have overridden the better promptings of his conscience with the result that he truly dishonors himself and is fatally wounded. The price of venging himself against Hamlet, as he soon realizes, is his own just destruction.

Though Hamlet is anxious to continue his fight with Laertes despite Claudius' attempts to have them parted, the fight is finally stopped by the fall of the Queen. Horatio also notes that "they bleed on both sides" and asks Hamlet how he is. Osric also asks Laertes how he is and Laertes replies: "Why, as a woodcock to mine own springe [trap], Osric. / I am justly killed with mine own treachery." Hamlet, not as seriously wounded as Laertes, is more concerned about his mother, but Claudius answers his query by saying that Gertrude is only swooning at the sight of their blood. When she hears Claudius' false words, the dying Gertrude cries out: "No, no, the drink, the drink! O my dear Hamlet / The drink, the drink! I am poisoned."

COMMENT: Though it must have been a terrible act of duplicity for Claudius to lie about his beloved wife's fatal condition, the lie does clear Gertrude's mind of her own delusions. She suddenly understands what has happened to her, that she has been poisoned by the drink prepared by her husband for her son and, what is even more important, that to protect himself Claudius allowed her to drink poison and is now lying to cover his guilt. In her final moments she fully faces the evil that she had tried to avoid seeing in Claudius and, allying herself completely with her son against this poisonous destroyer of her peace, her family and her life, she cries out his guilt for all to hear.

With the Queen's full confession of Claudius' villainy before the assembled court, the enraged Hamlet attempts to assume control of the state and begin an immediate inquiry into Claudius' guilt: "O villainy! Ho! let the door be locked. / Treachery! See it out." But Laertes now falls with the words, "Hamlet, thou art slain." He explains that the sword in Hamlet's hands is not only sharp but poisoned and that Hamlet has no more than "half an hour's life." Laertes is also doomed, for his "foul practice / Hath turned itself on me." For both their deaths and for the poisoning of the Queen,

104   H A M L E T

he cries out to all, "The king, the king's to blame." Hearing that his life is now forfeit, Hamlet turns his poisoned sword on the King with the words, "The point envenomed too? / Then, venom, to thy work." But though Claudius is apparently convicted by the reigning Queen and by Laertes of the "treacherous" murder of themselves and of the crown prince, so great is the court's horror of regicide and reverence for a King's life that they all cry out "Treason! treason!" against Hamlet's murderous act. At this cry of support from his court, the fatally poisoned Claudius speaks his last words, "O, yet defend me, friends, I am but hurt."

> **COMMENT:** Hamlet was just about to present his own evidence against Claudius in an official court of justice which he hoped would lead to the judicial execution of Claudius and his own assumption of rule when Laertes informed him that he was poisoned. But if Hamlet was not expecting to die, how much more dreadful is Claudius' state of spiritual unpreparedness. Having just wronged his beloved wife by blatantly lying about her condition, he now descends to the more desperate lie of self-delusion, saying that he is "but hurt." Unprepared to die, Claudius desperately clings to the delusion of possible life as before he had clung to the hope of preserving his throne while helplessly watching his wife die. Trying to play god to the end, he has only succeeded in destroying both his wife and himself.

But Hamlet quickly dispatches him with the poisoned drink he had prepared. Forcing this down his throat, he cries: "Here, thou incestuous, murd'rous, damned Dane, / Drink off this potion. Is thy union here? / Follow my mother." As the King dies, Laertes says that "he is justly served" by the poison he had prepared for Hamlet. He now turns to Hamlet with his last words: "Exchange forgiveness with me, noble Hamlet. / Mine and my father's death come not upon thee, / Nor thine on me!" The dying Hamlet accepts the dead Laertes' wish as he says: "Heaven make thee free of it! I follow thee."

> **COMMENT:** Hamlet had earlier referred to Laertes as "a very noble youth" and now Laertes fulfills that potential nobility which had been buried under the false honor of appearances he had learned from his father. He rises to the true reconciliation which Hamlet had earlier desired but which he had fatally delayed out of false pride and jealousy, and he, too, is won completely to Hamlet's side. This final movement of Gertrude and Laertes to Hamlet's side serves to redeem them from the guilt of their complicity with Claudius, if not to save their lives. But it also serves in the re-

habilitation of Hamlet in our eyes. Gertrude's "dear Hamlet" and Laertes' "noble Hamlet" remain our final image of Shakespeare's transformed hero.

Hamlet wishes he could more fully explain his act to the horrified spectators but, "as this fell sergeant, Death, / Is strict in his arrest," he tells Horatio that he must "report me and my cause aright / To the unsatisfied."

COMMENT: The most important thing about the accomplishment of Hamlet's "revenge" is that revenge for his father's murder is no longer the motive for his action. What finally unleashes Hamlet's lethal thrust is his recognition that he, himself, has fallen a mortal victim to Claudius' plot against him: "The point envenomed too? / Then, venom to thy work." Though he had meant to take judicial action against Claudius for his responsibility in the death of his mother and the plot against his own life, he now uses the little time left him to avenge his own murder, witnessed to before the court by Laertes' dying evidence against Claudius. After taking action on his own behalf with the weapon which had cost him his life, Hamlet turns to avenge his mother's death with the same drink which had poisoned her. Condemning Claudius for only those actions of which the court has objective knowledge, his incestuous marriage to his brother's widow and final murder of her before their eyes, for both of which he ought now to be "damned," Hamlet's final words to Claudius are: "Follow my mother."

But if Hamlet has finally caught Claudius in an act "that has no relish of salvation in't," as is proven by Claudius' state of spiritual unpreparedness for death, he, himself, has now transcended the earlier spirit of revenge which might also have caused his own damnation. He has not committed the premeditated revenge commanded by the ghost. Though the ghost's command unsettled his reason and led him to other acts of cruel death, for which he is now paying with his life, he has not acted upon the ghost's direct and possibly diabolic order for his father's revenge and, however shamed his sense of honor may have been by this delay, he has as well transcended his former allegiance to the honor code, now so thoroughly discredited by Laertes' conformity to its dictates. Moreover, it is only through this transcendence of the ultimately unchristian honor code that Hamlet rises to the height of true nobility, as is indicated by first Laertes and then Horatio's appellation of him as "noble." This noble transcendence of

the damnable dictates of honor was only accomplished, however, by his new understanding and final commitment to the
"divinity that shapes our ends." He had had faith that, without any direct planning on his part, heaven would so dispose
events that he would be able to fulfill its will and his own as
long as they remained in harmony. And events did so dispose
themselves to cause him once more to act "rashly," though
his spontaneous act against Claudius was undertaken in the
spirit of such "perfect conscience" that it could only appear
to objective viewers as the purest justice. Though it was at the
unfortunate cost of his own and his mother's lives, Hamlet
was thus able to execute Claudius in the most "perfect conscience" for these public events alone.

That the events which led Hamlet to this just execution of
Claudius also involved his own death and the deaths of his
mother and Laertes only shows the more clearly the working
of universal justice through them. Laertes judges that not only
is Claudius "justly served" but he, himself, is "justly killed
with mine own treachery." Though he excuses Hamlet's murder of Polonius on the grounds of madness which Hamlet
had offered, cosmic justice is less generous and has used this
same repentent Laertes to effect the final punishment of its
"scourge and minister," but this only after it has also allowed
him to achieve the highest development of man, that state
of "readiness," of true nobility, which must earn our admiration. And what of the Queen, left to heavenly justice? Cannot
the hand of heaven be traced in the "accidental" death she
willfully purchased through the poison prepared by the one
who had originally infected her? Though Ernest Jones may
find confirmation of his Freudian theory in the fact that,
because of his supposed subconscious identification with Claudius' crimes, Hamlet only kills Claudius when he himself is
dying, it seems clear that in Shakespeare's mind, as in Hamlet's, the explanation reaches beyond any such personality
defects or complexes into the very heart of a religious mystery.

For once, Horatio attempts to go against Hamlet's wishes. Objecting that he is "more an antique Roman than a Dane" (that is, a
Stoic who believes in suicide rather than survival with shame),
Horatio attempts to emulate Hamlet's nobility, as he understands
it, by drinking the remaining poison and following his beloved
friend to death. But with his last strength Hamlet forcibly wrests
the poisoned cup from Horatio's hands: "Give me the cup. Let go.
By heaven, I'll ha't." Death may provide final happiness, but if
Horatio truly loves him he would better follow his example by
continuing the painful process of living and justifying Hamlet's

name: "If thou didst ever hold me in thy heart, / Absent thee from felicity awhile, / And in this harsh world draw thy breath in pain, / To tell my story."

Hamlet now hears a "warlike noise" and is informed by Osric that it is the greeting of Fortinbras, returned from his conquest in Poland, to the ambassadors from England whom he has met on his way to Elsinore. The poison has so overcome him, however, that Hamlet fears he will not live long enough to hear the result of his substituted commission to the English King. As his death will also mark the end of the Danish royal line, he now turns his last thoughts to the question of the Danish succession, for he is now *de facto* ruler of Denmark and must attend to the good of his state: "I do prophesy th' election lights / On Fortinbras. He has my dying voice." Horatio is to tell Fortinbras of this and of all that has happened because for Hamlet "the rest is silence." As Hamlet dies, Horatio bids farewell to his noble friend in the full confidence of his spiritual salvation: "Now cracks a noble heart. Good night, sweet prince, / And flights of angels sing thee to thy rest!" Immediately upon the death of Hamlet, Fortinbras enters with the ambassadors from England.

COMMENT: The entrance of the ambassadors from England immediately following the close of the short "interim" time in which Hamlet was confident that he would end Claudius' life can only be viewed as Shakespeare's structural support for the validity of Hamlet's theological conclusions. If there was any question that such conclusions were no more than new rationalizations on Hamlet's part for his behavior, Shakespeare's dramatic plotting must give this the lie. The fact that without any plan Hamlet was exactly able to accomplish his purpose in the allowed time and do this more justly than he could have thought possible is proof that, within the universe of Shakespeare's play, Hamlet's insight into the nature of reality is as valid as it is profound. The moral significance of this new understanding is given further validity by the spiritual change it has worked in Hamlet. Though Hamlet still views the world as "harsh," as how should he not with such proof of the harsh workings of universal justice, he now rejects any suggestion of suicide, using his last strength to insist upon the necessity for Horatio to live, however painful it may be to continue to draw breath. And his own last thoughts are his most life affirming. He is concerned for the healthy continuance of the state whose evils he has scourged with such fatal consequences for himself. Though his life was tortured by the black vision of death, he dies with the dearly earned vision of the high value of life. Entirely purged of its evils, his spirit will not need to break its eternal "silence" as may have been the case with his father's spirit. Though dreadfully tempted by the powers of damnation, his spirit has most nobly won its salvation.

As Fortinbras views the royal deaths he can only ask, "O proud Death, / What feast is toward in thine eternal cell" (reminding us thereby of the equal validity of Hamlet's earlier if less graced vision of death's universal feeding upon man). To complete death's feast, the ambassador from England informs us "that Rosencrantz and Guildenstern are dead." Horatio now suggests that the bodies be arranged in state and placed on view after which he can tell them "Of carnal, bloody, and unnatural acts, / Of accidental judgments, casual slaughters, / Of deaths put on by cunning and forced cause, / And, in this upshot, purposes mistook / Fall'n on th' inventors' heads." Fortinbras is anxious to hear of this but also takes the opportunity to state his claim to the throne of Denmark. Horatio says that he has cause to speak of this as well but that first the funeral arrangement should be made to quiet "men's minds." Fortinbras now orders four captains to "bear Hamlet like a soldier" to a high platform accompanied by the rites of a military funeral, "For he was likely, had he been put on, / To have proved most royal." As the soldiers bear Hamlet upwards to the sounds of cannons, the tragedy comes to a fitting end.

CONCLUDING COMMENT: Horatio has spoken of two kinds of deaths, "of accidental judgments, casual slaughters," on the one hand, and, on the other, "of deaths put on by cunning and forced cause, / And, in this upshot, purposes mistook / Fall'n on th' inventors' heads." The first type characterizes the actions of Hamlet, whose killings have all been accidental or casual. The second type characterizes the "deep plots" of Claudius and Laertes, who have tried to shape their ends directly with the ironic result of punishing themselves and, in the case of Claudius, the one most dear to him. In either case we may equally see the hand of the "divinity that shapes our ends." Hamlet has allowed Providence to work itself out through him; Claudius and Laertes have tried to shape their own destinies and for this are punished. The distinction between them, however, raises Hamlet above Claudius and all his accomplices, whatever the extent of their complicity.

But if Hamlet deserves our admiration for his final "readiness" to accept and further the will of heaven, his life also stands forfeit for the bloody course he has traveled to this end. It is this tension between earthly defeat and spiritual redemption which makes Hamlet's death truly tragic. For at the very moment when he has finally achieved a full "readiness" for a noble life, when "he was likely, had he been put on, / To have proved most royal," his life is over. Though we mourn the tragic waste of his potential, hindered from its continuance by the fatal interaction of the tragic flaws in his personality and his world, we must also glory that he has won a victory in defeat, seeing with Hamlet that "the readiness is all."

CHARACTER ANALYSES

HAMLET   Hamlet dares us, along with Rosencrantz and Guildenstern, to "pluck out the heart of my mystery." This mystery marks the essence of Hamlet's character as, in spite of our popular psychologies, it ultimately does for all human personalities. Granting this, we can attempt to chart its origin and outward manifestations. Ophelia tells us that before the events of the play Hamlet was a model courtier, soldier and scholar, "The glass of fashion and the mould of form, / Th' observed of all observers." With the death of his father and the hasty, incestuous remarriage of his mother to his uncle, however, Hamlet is thrown into a suicidal frame of mind in which "the uses of this world" seem to him "weary, stale, flat, and unprofitable." Though his faith in the value of life has been destroyed by this double confrontation with death and human infidelity, he feels impotent to effect any change in this new reality: "It is not, nor it cannot come to good. / But break my heart, for I must hold my tongue." All he can do in this frustrated state is to lash out with bitter satire at the evils he sees and then relapse into suicidal melancholy.

It is in this state that he meets the equally mysterious figure of his father's ghost with its supernatural revelations of murder and adultery and its injunction upon Hamlet to revenge his father's murder. While this command gives purpose and direction to Hamlet's hitherto frustrated impulse towards scourging reform, it also serves to further unsettle his already disturbed reason. When two months later he forces his way into Ophelia's room, he looks "As if he had been loosed out of hell / To speak of horrors." Whether or not the ghost was actually a devil, its effect upon Hamlet has been diabolic.

In the two months after his meeting with the ghost, he puzzles the court with his assumed madness but does nothing concrete to effect or further his revenge. His inability to either accept the goodness of life or act to destroy its evils now begins to trouble him as much as his outward hysteria and depression does the court. He first condemns his apparent lack of concentration on his revenge as the sign of a base, cowardly nature. The advent of a company of players, however, gives him an idea for testing the truth of the ghost and the guilt of Claudius. Rationalizing his inactivity as an effect of his doubt about the ghost's nature, he plans to have the players perform a play which reproduces Claudius' crime and observe Claudius' reaction to it, thereby dispelling his own

110

doubts as to the proper course of his action. Having momentarily silenced his shame at his inaction, however, he immediately relapses into his former state; he meditates upon suicide and then lashes out with satiric cruelty at Ophelia.

The performance of the play is successful in revealing Claudius' guilt to Hamlet, and Hamlet reacts to this proof with wild glee. His old friends Rosencrantz and Guildenstern, who had returned that day to Elsinore to help further Claudius' investigation into Hamlet's disorder and had thereby alienated Hamlet's affections, enter with a message from Hamlet's mother that she wishes to see him immediately. Hamlet treats them contemptuously before returning his answer that he will go to his mother. His coming visit with his mother inspires him with a murderous rage appropriate to the hellish time of night. Once more in the power of hell, he accidentally comes upon the praying figure of Claudius but does not take this opportunity for revenge because of the devilish rationalization that such revenge would not damn Claudius' soul. But the truth seems to be that Hamlet's murderous rage is misdirected at his mother rather than at Claudius, even though Hamlet is now fully convinced of his guilt. Coming to his mother's room with the intent to punish her with verbal daggers for her unfaithfulness, her unwillingness to listen to him releases his murderous impulse against her. In a moment of temporary insanity he manages to exercise enough control to deflect the blow designed for her to the direction of an unexpected sound, killing the hidden figure of Polonius. In the ensuing scene he all but forgets the body of Polonius in his urgency to arouse his mother's guilt for her treatment of his father and injury to his own trust.

This fact, together with his obsessed preoccupation with his mother's sexual life, may provide a clue to the "mystery" of Hamlet. Hamlet, himself, had admitted to Ophelia that women's sensual falseness "hath made me mad." Elaborating on this clue, Ernest Jones has provided a well-reasoned Freudian explanation of Hamlet's behavior, namely the reactivation of his repressed Oedipus Complex. But whatever the truth of the matter, Hamlet's intuition does not extend this far. All he knows is that his mother's behavior has contributed to wrenching the time "out of joint" for him, and that he has been fated "to set it right."

Once he is reconciled to his mother, the whole of reality appears to him in a different light. Where before his will was "most incorrect to heaven," the "Everlasting" seeming to be the creator of sterile farces and imposer of harsh laws, he now can accept heaven's purposes and ally himself with them as heaven's "scourge and minister." If Hamlet's nausea with life as well as sex seems to the modern intelligence to have a hidden psychological basis, Hamlet raises the discussion of his nature to the ultimately more profound level of religious existential confrontation. Seeing the hand of heaven in his accidental slaying of Polonius as well as in the exile to England which will result from it, he is able to accept this turn of events with new confidence in his ultimate success.

Though Hamlet does not appear outwardly changed, as witnessed by his contemptuous treatment of Polonius' body, continued obsession with the horror of death and with the obligations of honor, the change in attitude begun in his mother's room continues to develop while on shipboard and is responsible for his actions there. Inspired by his restlessness, he rashly discovers the letter ordering his death, forges a new commission which substitutes for his death the deaths of Claudius' accomplices, Rosencrantz and Guildenstern, returns the commission unknown, and, in a sea fight with pirates, manages to free himself from the Danish ship. In all of this he sees "heaven ordinant" and this teaches him that "There's a divinity that shapes our ends, / Rough-hew them how we will." Recognizing by this that humanly conceived plots are doomed to fail, he places himself completely in the hands of Providence.

Nonetheless, his first actions upon his return do not seem to indicate any real change in his nature from our last view of him in Denmark. He is still overly sensitive to the decomposition of the body after death and, in his treatment of Laertes at the funeral he so rudely disrupts, he still shows a cruel insensitivity to the feelings of anyone he believes to have wronged him. This insensitivity also extends to his lack of any qualms about his murders of Rosencrantz and Guildenstern, as was also true of his earlier murder of Polonius. If Hamlet had once been a model human being disillusioned in life by the double blows of his father's death and mother's remarriage, his oversensitivity to these evils of existence has warped his nature into an equally extreme insensitivity to all those whom he suspects of impurity. He cruelly torments his mother and Ophelia, bitterly mocks Polonius, Rosencrantz and Guildenstern and then wantonly kills them without a qualm and with the attempt, in the last two cases, of ensuring their eternal damnation, and he refrains from killing Claudius for this same evil reason. In terms of vindictive cruelty and wanton slaughter, he stands far more condemned for evil than Claudius and in danger of his own eternal damnation.

This warping of a sensitive nature into one capable of inhuman evil is perhaps the clearest proof of the evils of existence, though Hamlet must now be numbered among the evils to be punished by cosmic justice. But if Hamlet's actions condemn him to death, his growing perception of reality finally redeems his soul in our eyes. Though Claudius has planned Hamlet's destruction and Hamlet has proof of this, he has returned to Denmark without any plan for his revenge, even warning Claudius rudely of his approach. In "perfect conscience" now about the sin of regicide, he is confident that, in the "interim" before the arrival of the English ambassadors, heaven will so dispose events that he will be able to execute Claudius without any prior planning.

And his belief in the providential control of all events is justified by the outcome. Claudius' responsibility for Hamlet's death and the death of his mother is established before the court by Laertes and he is able to execute Claudius for these crimes alone. Hamlet has transcended his earlier damnable intention of premeditated revenge in a spontaneous act of just repayment for the loss of his own life. Recognizing that "the readiness is all," Hamlet has finally achieved this readiness to endure both life and death. His final actions are his most life affirming, his restraining of Horatio from committing suicide and his concern for the continuing welfare of Denmark. The tragedy of his death is that it comes at the moment when "he was likely, had he been put on, / To have proved most royal." Destroyed and redeemed by the same brilliance of perception, Hamlet's spirit has undergone a tragic development from the self-destructive negation of life and of heaven's purposes to a new affirmation of the providential sanctity of life, and it is this final "readiness" which redeems him.

CLAUDIUS At the beginning of the play, Claudius is a man who has achieved his heart's desire and is fully confident of his ability to preserve his position. If it cost him any pain to commit adultery with his brother's wife and then kill him, this cost is now forgotten in the happy possession of his crown and beloved Queen. But this possession required more than criminal daring than knowing what he wanted and taking it. If he was not an able politician, his murder would not have assured him election to the throne over the pretensions of his nephew, Hamlet. If he was not an attractive person, he could never have won the sentimentally conventional Gertrude to his adulterous love. Now that he has his throne and Queen he wants only peace to enjoy them. In an admirable diplomatic move, he averts war with Norway. In his more personal diplomacy, he wins the support of the chief counselors of state for all of his plans and tries most earnestly to win the goodwill of Hamlet by requesting that he remain in Denmark to enjoy his royal favor. He believes in making the best of a difficult situation and preaches such acceptance to Hamlet.

But if Hamlet was still in conspicuous mourning two months after his father's death and appeared to grudge Claudius his throne and marriage, in four months time his behavior has become dangerously provocative. Anxious to overcome this single impediment to his security and the smooth functioning of his state, Claudius sets spies on Hamlet to try to understand what is troubling him. Rosencrantz and Guildenstern can tell him nothing, but the scene he witnesses between Hamlet and Ophelia, in which Hamlet seemed to threaten his life, convinces him that he must act immediately to protect himself, and he decides to do this by sending Hamlet off to England for a time.

Though he has controlled himself very well up until this time, his composure breaks down when, through the performance of the play ordered by Hamlet and Hamlet's accompanying remarks, he faces the incredible fact that Hamlet has exact knowledge of his crime against Hamlet's father and is dedicated to revenge it. But though a cool, criminal head would dictate Hamlet's destruction, Claudius is instead plunged into spiritual despair. All his hidden guilt now comes to the surface and, rather than add a new crime to his conscience, Claudius' only concern is to try to repent his former sins and so win the salvation of his soul. This is very difficult for him because he knows it would require him to confess his sins, give up his crown and Queen and face possible execution. Moreover, he loves Gertrude so profoundly that he cannot bear her loss. He is a man in love with life, pleasure and especially power and he only wishes to be able to enjoy them and to use them well. But Hamlet has so succeeded in arousing his guilt that all of this seems nothing beside the sin of brother murder by which he gained them. Despite even his own nature, then, he desperately prays for the grace which would enable him to give up his worldly pleasures and achieve spiritual peace. Though his ties to crown and Queen are too strong to permit this total renunciation, the extent of his guilt and hesitance to proceed further into crime reveal a nature not essentially evil.

Claudius is a man capable of deep love, hearty enjoyment and a beneficial use of power. He wants nothing more than to win the love and admiration of all and, even in the face of Hamlet's rudest provocations, manages to maintain a cordial politeness and concern. His only flaw is that he feels himself entitled to more than his given portion and there is no inner hindrance to prevent his taking it. Though he preaches the acceptance of his evil as the will of heaven, he was unable to accept the heavenly dispensation which gave his brother everything that he, himself, desired; and so he made himself the god of his own universe and celebrates his power with the earthly thunder of cannons. Hamlet's insane killing of Polonius, however, puts an end to Claudius' hesitation. He can no longer deny Hamlet's extreme danger to him and self preservation overrides the objections of his conscience and his loving concern for Gertrude's peace of mind. But as his conscience was strong enough to arouse his guilt but not sufficiently powerful to cause him to forego his life and happiness, so now it does not prevent him from planning Hamlet's murder but makes him too squeamish to perform it himself. He plots to convert Hamlet's exile into his death, though he does not stop to consider how he will later answer for this death. And when this plot fails, he immediately plans another, this time using Laertes instead of the King of England as his instrument. Again the plot is conceived in too desperate a state to really mark its consequences, and this time its failure is so awful that it involves the accidental death of his beloved wife and his own final end.

Relying upon his continuing ability to shape his destiny, Claudius piles misconceived plot upon plot in a desperate attempt to preserve his ill-gotten gains. Though he keeps his head when Laertes threatens his throne and, more fearfully, when Gertrude drinks the poison he had prepared for Hamlet, he is so concerned to preserve his life that he has forgotten his soul. He has missed the opportunity of repenting his former sins and when he dies nonetheless, it is in the act of piling more crimes and lies upon his unprepared soul. He had earlier explained that his reason for not taking direct action against Hamlet was "that my arrows, / Too slightly timbered for so loud a wind, / Would have reverted to my bow again, / And not where I had aimed them." And so has it also been of the puny plots by which he hoped to outwit the "divinity that shapes our ends."

GERTRUDE The beloved wife and mother of the "mighty opposites" of the play, who is largely responsible for Hamlet's anguished inability to proceed with his revenge and Claudius' hesitation to preserve himself through the destruction of Hamlet, she who was "my virtue or my plague, be it either which," for both of her loves, is herself a most ordinary creature. Beautiful and warm-hearted, she has no mind of her own and is pulled by whatever force is most powerfully directed at her at any moment. By temperament she turns to the sunny side of life and cannot bear to face any pain or conflict. What pain her adultery with Claudius may have cost her we cannot know though we can guess it may have provided the most urgent motivation for his murder of her husband. That he so carefully concealed the knowledge of his crime from her is further indication of her lack of criminal daring and of his concern for her peace of mind. When circumstances so worked out that she was able to marry her lover, however, she was most happy and desired only that all the difficulties of the past be forgotten.

Hamlet's refusal to forget the death of his father or to forgive her hasty and incestuous remarriage is the only blot on her happiness; it continues to remind her of the continuing difficulties of her

position which she had naively hoped would be ended by her restoration to the conventionally accepted state of marriage. If she
could only get Hamlet to accept her new husband as his new father,
she could completely bury the past in the happy present. She therefore begs him to remain at Elsinore so that this reconciliation can
take place. But as she watches her beloved and remarkable son
only become more and more mentally deranged with the passing
months and sees his provocative behavior beginning to upset even
the composure of Claudius, her happiness becomes increasingly
blighted. She hopes that Rosencrantz and Guildenstern will be
able to bring him out of his depression. Then she snatches at the
possibility that Hamlet's disturbance might actually be caused by
his love for Ophelia rather than her own behavior and hopes that
Ophelia will be able to cure him. Her spirits rise for a moment
when she sees Hamlet's excited involvement with the play and his
attentions to Ophelia, but then they immediately drop as Claudius
rises from the performance in anguish. Finally she is prevailed
upon by Polonius to do that which she has avoided for all these
months, to meet Hamlet privately to discuss his behavior and try to
understand its source. And it is probably only as the last resort
to the exiling of Hamlet that she permits this dreaded meeting at all.

Hamlet's immediate charge, "Mother, you have my father much
offended," confirms her worst fears of her own responsibility for
Hamlet's state, and she tries to put a quick end to the interview
rather than have to face his further condemnation. But she is
shocked into submission by the murderous rage he displays towards
her and finally releases onto the hidden figure of Polonius. To
Hamlet's continuing insults, she first answers in the pride of an
innocent conscience: "What have I done that thou dar'st wag thy
tongue / In noise so rude against me?" Her avoidance of self
scrutiny is so complete, that she really believes that she has nothing
to answer for beyond the unfortunate effect her hasty remarriage
has had upon her son. But as Hamlet continues to compel her
attention to the horror of her remarriage, she gradually comes under
his spell and begins to experience a new guilt for her actions.
Though the entrance of the ghost, which she cannot see, convinces
her that Hamlet is mad and his abuse the product of an overwrought
moral sensibility, she cannot fully undo the sense of guilt he has
aroused in her.

When Ophelia goes mad, Gertrude wishes to avoid the painful
sight of her as much as she had earlier wished to avoid looking
into her own soul. This is especially so since Gertrude sees Ophelia's
mental breakdown as further proof of the continuing evil caused by
her unthinking behavior, and this chain of evil effects seems, to
her guilty conscience, to bode some great catastrophe. Though
deeply grieved by Ophelia's death, she tries, nonetheless, to explain

it to herself and to Laertes in the least damaging way. But her sorrow at Ophelia's funeral is accentuated by the madness her son displays there in his unexpected return. His insulting behavior to Laertes, who has already felt himself sufficiently wronged by Hamlet to demand revenge, now so worries her that she sends word to Hamlet that he should excuse himself to Laertes and try to regain his goodwill.

When Hamlet appears at the fencing match in such a reasonable frame of mind, she is delighted. Not only does Laertes appear to accept Hamlet's offer of love, but Hamlet's own willingness to fight as Claudius' champion seems to promise her their reconciliation as well. If Laertes were reconciled to Hamlet and Hamlet to Claudius, all the horror of her guilt and Ophelia's death might yet be forgotten and she might still be granted the happiness that she had thought Ophelia's marriage to Claudius would bring her. In this blind hope of future happiness, her son's gentlemanly behavior and excellence of fencing so intoxicate her that she joins fully into the event, coming forward to wipe her dear boy's brow and finally insisting upon toasting his coming victory. Against Claudius' objection, she drinks to her son to show him how happy he has made her.

As she has ever evaded the prospect of anything painful in the hope of achieving happiness, so it is fitting that this flaw should prove her destruction. Only as she feels the poison creeping over her and hears her husband lie about her condition to save himself does she truly face reality. Only then does she begin to understand Hamlet's objections to Claudius and recognize that Claudius has poisoned her whole life as now he has her body. Trying too late to protect her "dear Hamlet," she dies the miserable victim of her sentimental and deluded hope for happiness.

POLONIUS The Lord Chamberlain and chief courtier at Elsinore, Polonius appears to have been flattered into giving his support to Claudius. At any rate, this flattery, which probably gained Claudius his election to the throne, is poured on him by Claudius when we first view him. But Claudius' flattery is nothing to Polonius' self-flattery. He detains his son Laertes' departure, which he had come to hurry, with a set of old saws about proper behavior which have nothing to do with his own behavior but which he rattles off as a mark of his elderly wisdom. Old he is and so proud of his apparent wisdom that, upon learning of his daughter Ophelia's involvement with Hamlet, he immediately decides that Hamlet's intentions must be dishonorable and forbids his too innocent daughter from seeing him again. Judging both Hamlet and Laretes by his own youthful indulgences, he not only prejudges Hamlet's interest in his daughter but sends his servant, Reynaldo, to spy upon Laertes in Paris. He is at his height as he explains the refinements of spying to Reynaldo and cares nothing that in his concern to find out the worst about his son he may actually be hurting Laertes' reputation. Though he seems almost to encourage tight leash, demanding her confidences, telling her what to think his son to take some youthful liberties, he keeps his daughter on a and how to act. Whatever spirit she might have had he has apparently broken, molding her into a model daughter of silent, mindless obedience. (One wonders if such an upbringing might also explain Gertrude's lack of moral independence.)

Like a dutiful daughter, Ophelia comes immediately to her father to report Hamlet's strange behavior upon forcing himself into her room. As quickly as he had assumed Hamlet's dishonorable intentions, so now he decides that it was true love and that Ophelia's rejection of him has driven him mad. He now admits that his earlier orders to Ophelia were lacking in sound judgment but sets his authoritarian presumption down to the natural effects of age. Seeing in Ophelia's relationship to Hamlet a way to further endear himself to the King and perhaps offset any other adverse effects his age may have had against him, he immediately takes his trembling daughter off to the King.

The ludicrous effects of his age soon make themselves apparent in the long-winded, pretentious way he takes to get to the point. With no concern for his daughter's feelings, he proceeds to read a love letter Hamlet had written to her, making literary comments on Hamlet's style all the while. Having interested the King and Queen in his theory of Hamlet's madness, he now further plans to prostitute his daughter's modesty to gain the King's favor by suggesting that a meeting be arranged between his daughter and Hamlet which the king and he would spy upon. In fact, so sure is he of his theory and, through it, of his continuing usefulness to the King that he arrogantly asserts that they can behead him or send him off to keep a farm if he is wrong. All of this does indicate, of course, a growing insecurity about his position in the state since his recent blunder with his daughter.

He now tries to investigate Hamlet himself, though Hamlet only makes fun of him in the most contemptuous way. Though he sets all of Hamlet's remarks about his old age down to madness, he is yet forced to admit, "Though this be madness, yet there is method in't." When the players come he again takes the opportunity to be with Hamlet and, as Hamlet and the players recite certain speeches, he is pleased once more to offer them his critical opinions on the verse and their acting. After conveying to Claudius Hamlet's invitation to a performance of a play that evening, he directs his daughter to her own performance for Hamlet's benefit as well as their own; she is to excuse her lonely presence at the arranged spot with a show of pious meditation. Though in the ensuing scene Hamlet treats Ophelia cruelly, Polonius is too concerned with the King to pay her much attention. All his concern is now to maintain his privileged position at court as Chief Counselor to the King. Since, despite his own opinion to the contrary, Claudius no longer will entertain his theory of Hamlet's madness and decides to send Hamlet off to England, Polonius now suggests a new spying plan to Claudius which might vindicate his own theory or reveal a new solution to their dilemmas: after the performance of the play, the Queen should send to Hamlet for a private conference in her room, and he will himself hide in her room the better to report the conclusion to Claudius. At the play performance he is quick to point out to Claudius Hamlet's attentions to Ophelia as further support to the wisdom of his theory. And after the play he cannot rely upon Rosencrantz and Guildenstern to get Hamlet to Gertrude's room but comes himself to hurry Hamlet. Then, quickly reporting his success to Claudius, he rushes to Gertrude's room, gives her final instructions on how to deal with Hamlet and hides himself.

But the overanxious, presumptuous and self-deluding fool has blundered again. Concerned only with his own self importance and incapable of taking the measure of one like Hamlet, he precipitates a situation which ends with his own accidental death. Hamlet speaks the most fitting closing description of him when he says: "Thou wretched, rash, intruding fool, farewell!" But if Polonius' efforts on behalf of his children have been as damaging to them as they have been on his own behalf, their effects live on beyond him. Lost without the father upon whom she had obediently depended for her every thought and act, Ophelia loses her mind and meets her death. And the false and outward sense of honor Polonius has implanted in Laertes causes him to try to revenge his father's death in a most underhanded way and leads to his own death as well. As poor a counselor to himself as he was to others, we must finally agree with Hamlet: "Indeed, this counsellor / Is now most still, most secret, and most grave, / Who was in life a foolish prating knave."

OPHELIA   "Pretty Ophelia," as Claudius calls her, is the most innocent victim of Hamlet's revenge. Attracted by her sweet beauty after the depressing event of his father's death, Hamlet had fallen in love with her. She had "sucked the honey of his music vows" and returned his affection. But when her father had challenged the honor of Hamlet's intentions, Ophelia could only reply: "I do not know, my lord, what I should think." Used to relying upon her father's direction and brought up to be obedient, she can only accept her father's belief, seconded by that of her brother, that

Hamlet's "holy vows" of love were simply designed for her seduction and obey her father's orders not to permit Hamlet to see her again.

When his mother's hasty remarriage had led Hamlet to the disillusioned view that "frailty, thy name is woman," Ophelia's affection might yet have restored his spirit. But her unexplained refusal to see him soon after his mother's remarriage completes Hamlet's disillusionment with women. The ghost's revelation that his mother had not only dishonored his father's memory but also their marriage by her adultery with Claudius festers in his mind for two months until he finally forces his way into Ophelia's room to look upon her again. Searching her innocent face for some sign of loving truth that might restore his faith in her and, through her, in womankind and in love, he takes her mute terror for a further sign of her guilt and sees her as but another false Gertrude. And, indeed, there is much similarity between the two women in his life and in the play. Both are beautiful and rather simple minded women, easily molded by the more powerful opinions and desires of others. Perhaps it was this similarity which first attracted Hamlet to Ophelia as now it disenchants him with her. They are the same type of woman at different stages of life. But Ophelia is still too much under the influence of her father to question his wisdom or authority, and she has no mind of her own to understand how she has made her lover suffer. As she could not believe that her father's orders were wrong, no matter how much it pained her not to see Hamlet, so all she can see in his present behavior is the madness of which the whole court is talking and which terrifies her. Though her father admits that he had made a mistake in questioning the depth of Hamlet's love, she still does not dare to question his authority as he takes her precious love letters to the King and then orders her to meet Hamlet at a place where he and the King can observe their meeting. Her hopes for this meeting are raised, however, by the Queen's kind statement to her that she hopes Ophelia will prove to be the cause of Hamlet's madness for then there would be the hope that Ophelia might cure him and that they might be married. Though her father's admission of error and the Queen's blessing for her marriage might have embittered a more independent Ophelia towards her father for having hindered her love and turned her lover against her, Ophelia still accepts his guidance in a hopeful spirit. Hamlet's actions in her room, though deranged, show that he still loves her. Now her father is permitting her to see Hamlet once more and she has the Queen's blessing for her possible cure of and marriage to Hamlet. Like Gertrude, she hopes that all might yet be well, and she has even taken it upon herself to bring all of Hamlet's presents to this meeting in the hope of reawakening his love.

But after a hopeful beginning, Ophelia ruins her chances by the foolish feminine strategy of accusing Hamlet of rejecting her. This only enrages him against her duplicity and he cruelly denies ever having loved or given her anything. He then launches an ever more savage attack against her, telling her to enter a nunnery or else marry with his curse upon her. As this savage attack proceeds, Ophelia is again convinced of his madness and her hopes sink to despairing prayers to heaven to restore him. As she sees what has happened to her noble lover and to her earlier hopes for their love, she is overcome by her woe. At the play that evening he comes to sit by her, but whatever joy this might have given her is blasted by the disrespectful and vulgar way that he jokes with her. No longer addressing her "with love / In honorable fashion," he treats her like his familiar whore. When that night her father is mysteriously killed and then obscurely buried in great haste it is too much for her. Abused by her lover, bereft of her father's protection, alone and overcome by the sense of her dishonor and that of her father, she loses control of her mind.

In her insane state she comes to believe that that which her family tried so hard to protect her from, her seduction, has come to pass and that this explains Hamlet's rejection of her. Feeling by this the hypocrisy of the world and tormented by the vision of death and burial, she reaches out to the remaining loveliness of flowers and, in her careless attempt to hang them upon a sorrowing willow tree, somehow drowns. In an almost ironic repayment for her failure to understand what he has suffered, Hamlet has unthinkingly created a situation for her which parallels his own, death of a father and betrayal by a loved one. But whereas he managed to maintain final control over his sanity and rise above the temptation of suicide, her weaker spirit, unable to bear up under the burden of sorrow and disillusionment, finds its release in insanity and final death. That weakness of mind and will which permitted her obedience to her father and thus destroyed her hope in Hamlet's love finally results in her insanity and death.

LAERTES Laertes is a young man whose good instincts have been somewhat obscured by the concern with superficial appearances which he has imbibed from his father, Polonius. After a brief appearance at court to beg Claudius' leave to return to Paris, we see him again pompously lecturing his sister Ophelia about men's hypocritical ways and warning her to protect her chasity against "Hamlet, and the trifling of his favor." With some apparent knowledge of her brother's ways, she replies that he should not preach strictness to her while himself acting like a "reckless libertine." This suspicion of his behavior is later strengthened by Polonius' interest in spying upon Laertes' libertine habits in Paris. Like his father, Laertes apparently preaches a morality he does not practice and fully believes in a double standard of behavior for the sexes. But if his father allows him these liberties, it is that he may better approximate the manner of a so-called gentleman. More concerned with the outward signs of gentility than with any inner refinement of spirit, Laertes has well observed his father's advice to be concerned with appearances since "the apparel oft proclaims the man."

When he learns of his father's unexplained death and obscure funeral, Laertes' superficial sense of honor is touched to the quick. Since honor demands that he revenge his father's death, he returns to Denmark, gathers a rabble mob together and storms the castle, demanding that the King answer for his father's death. As unconcerned for the order of society as he is for his own salvation, he would rather "dare damnation" than leave his father's honor and his own besmirched. Though the sight of his sister's madness brings him to a moment of true grief, he is still primarily enraged by his father's "obscure funeral—-/ No trophy, sword, nor hatchment o'er his bones, / No noble rite nor formal ostentation." When Claudius explains Hamlet's responsibility for Polonius' death and his own reasons for covering up this fact, Laertes is satisfied to work with Claudius to achieve his revenge against Hamlet. Since he would be willing "to cut his throat i' th' church" to prove his honor, he is willing to stoop to any underhanded plan of Claudius' by which he can have his revenge. In fact, he even improves upon Claudius' suggestion for an illegally sharpened sword to be used in a fencing contest with Hamlet; Laertes volunteers to anoint the sword's point with poison, "that, if I gall him slightly, / It may be death." To vindicate his honor, he stoops to a most dishonorable practice.

If there was any chance of his renouncing such a dishonorable plan, Hamlet's behavior at his sister's funeral puts a quick end to this. Though his grief may take an ostentatious form, Hamlet's challenge to his rght to grieve, his fight with him in the very grave and then his insulting remarks upon leaving only re-enforce Laertes' resolution. Still, there was an opportunity during the scene for Laertes to achieve his revenge in the spirit of true honor. When Hamlet responds to Laertes' curses by offering him a duel to the death, Laertes might have accepted this offer and tried to achieve his revenge in a fair manner. But Hamlet's self-righteous behavior so outrages Laertes that his sense of honor becomes completely warped by his hatred for Hamlet and he cannot afford to take his chances with him.

One final opportunity is given to Laertes to act with true honor. When, at the start of the fencing match, Hamlet excuses his behavior at the funeral and his accidental slaying of Polonius on the grounds of his madness and asks for Laertes' pardon, Laertes has an opportunity to renounce his plan of revenge. Indeed, Hamlet's explanation and gentlemanly behavior towards him satisfies his natural feeling of vengeance. But Laertes is so concerned about his formal and outward "terms of honor" that he cannot permit his natural feelings to rule his will. In this concern for outward honor he further dishonors himself by the false statement that he will act honorably with Hamlet. Saying that "I do receive your offered love like love, / And will not wrong it," he goes and chooses the lethally sharp and poisoned weapon. Still, Hamlet's behavior towards him has been so gentlemanly that he cannot bring himself to dishonor his own word, and so fights poorly with Hamlet on the first two rounds, permitting Hamlet two easy hits against him. When the King chides him for his performance, he admits to himself that to kill Hamlet under these circumstances "is almost against my conscience." But when Hamlet begins to taunt him for his poor performance, it is too much for Laertes' pride. Playing as best he can, he is astonished to find that he can only bring Hamlet to a draw. His vengeance now enraged by jealousy at Hamlet's fine sportsmanship and true gentlemanly bearing, he lunges at Hamlet after the close of the formal bout and manages to wound him. When, by his wound, Hamlet realizes Laertes' false practice, he returns to the fight with such power that he captures Laertes' foil and wounds him fatally with it.

Had Laertes acted upon the honorable promptings of his conscience, he would have avoided his own death and, by allying himself with Hamlet, would have won the gratitude of the future King. Laertes' testimony of Claudius' responsibility for the poisoning of the Queen would have permitted Hamlet his just revenge against Claudius and would have left both Hamlet and Laertes alive. But Laertes' false sense of honor and pride override his better instincts to the fatal harm of both. Recognizing his dishonor too late and admitting that he is "justly killed with mine own treachery," Laertes finally rises to the true honor of admitting his fault to Hamlet, informing him of Claudius' designs, and then, in a tragically belated reconciliation with Hamlet, offering him an exchange of forgiveness. But if his rise to true honor finally redeems him in our eyes, his false honor has destroyed his life.

ROSENCRANTZ AND GUILDENSTERN Shakespeare's doubling of the type of courtier represented by both Rosencrantz and Guildenstern shows the tragic lack of individuality which this type possesses. They so revere their King that they are willing "to lay our service freely at your feet, / To be commanded." But Claudius' employment of them seems perfectly consistent with their honor. They are to try to interest their old but much changed friend Hamlet in some pleasures which might dispel his depression and also try to understand its cause that Claudius might be able to remedy it. Hamlet's most friendly greeting to them gives them hope

of early success and they immediately suggest that his depression is
caused by ambition. Hamlet denies this but it causes him to wonder
why they have come to Elsinore. When they reply that they have
come "To visit you, my lord; no other occasion," Hamlet finally
demands that they tell him directly whether or not they were sent
for. Unused to lying though honoring their royal commission, they
are unsure of how to answer. Finally their friendship for Hamlet
prevails and they admit, "My lord, we were sent for." But it is
too late. Hamlet already has "an eye of you" and will no further
trust them. Their momentary hesitance to be honest with Hamlet
has alienated his affection. And the passing of time only serves to
increase his enmity. Though they are intelligent enough for Hamlet
to share some general confession of his spiritual state with them
and for him to engage in pleasant conversation with them about
the latest theatrical news from Wittenburg, the open hearted gener-
osity with which he greeted them is now a thing of the past.

They immediately report the ill success of their interview and then
are soon employed again to bring Hamlet to his mother's room
after the performance of the play. The King's disturbance followed
by Hamlet's wild behavior upon their return to him further convince them of Claudius' just concern over Hamlet's dangerous condition. They therefore intensify their investigation of Hamlet's
admittedly "diseased" mind. This further antagonizes Hamlet so
that he throws their own suspicions back at them, saying, "Sir, I
lack advancement." Finally he becomes so annoyed by their attempts
to "pluck out the heart of my mystery" that he uses the recorders
to make fun of them in a most contemptuous manner. Hamlet's
belligerence towards them further alienates them from him and
draws them closer to the King. Fully convinced now of the danger
his madness poses to the King, their concern for the King's safety
becomes paramount. Accepting the common Renaissance belief that
the King is divinely appointed to rule the state for its own good,
they accept their dependence upon the King as the divinely sanc-
tioned order of nature. When the King now orders them to accom-
pany Hamlet on his voyage to England, a voyage which Claudius
says he hopes will cure Hamlet's disturbance, they are only too
willing to comply. By this means they may both help their friend
and protect their King. But when they learn of Hamlet's insane
killing of Polonius, they become fully committed to the welfare of
the King. Sent to find the body and bring Hamlet to the King, they
treat Hamlet in a high-handed manner. Hamlet reacts to their
manner by condemning them as courtiers wholly without integrity
who are willing to do anything commanded of them by the King
in the hope of reward but who will finally be unrewarded because
of their lack of character. He submits himself to their control with
full enmity of spirit. When aboard ship Hamlet discovers that the
commission they are carrying demands his death, he condemns them

without a hearing as criminal accomplices of a criminal King and sentences them to death "not shriving time allowed." Though Rosencrantz and Guildenstern are not conscious criminals, since they are unaware of the criminal designs of the King they obey, the fact that "they did make love to this employment" without any scrutiny into the King's purposes does condemn them as unthinking accomplices. If as model courtiers they feel they have nothing on their consciences, their lack of individual integrity and total dependence upon the King dooms them to the fate of the King to whom they are thus "mortised and adjoined."

HORATIO   Unlike Laertes, who had returned for Claudius' coronation and then left Elsinore for Paris, and unlike Rosencrantz and Guildenstern, who had not come for the royal events but had been sent for to investigate Hamlet, Horatio returns to Elsinore from Wittenburg for the funeral of Hamlet's father and remains to become Hamlet's one true friend. When Marcellus brings this university scholar to witness the sight of the ghost, with which the sentinels do not understand how to deal, he reports this event not to Claudius but to Hamlet. Although a courtier would have gone directly to the King, the blunt soldiers, Bernardo, Francisco and Marcellus, try to understand the matter for themselves and Horatio, whom they have sent for to this end, decides on his own judgment that this knowledge is for Hamlet's ears rather than the King's.

Horatio had come to see the ghost in a spirit of scepticism but, when he could not deny his own eyes, he carefully addressed the ghost in such a way as not to endanger his soul. When he comes to the same battlement the next night with Hamlet, he warns Hamlet not to follow the ghost as it might lead him into madness and suicide. After Hamlet's hysterical return from his conference with the ghost, Horatio tries to calm his spirit. He wins enough confidence from Hamlet for him to admit to Horatio that "it is an honest ghost," and later to generalize that "There are more things in heaven and earth, Horatio, / Than are dreamt of in your philosophy." He then swears Horatio and the soldiers to kep the knowledge of the ghost and of Hamlet's further purposes confidential, and they never break this confidence.

During the next two months Horatio's integrity and emotional reserve so win Hamlet's admiration that he fully takes him to his heart. Here is a friend whose integrity he can fully trust and whose Stoic reserve acts to calm his own passionate response to evil. He takes Horatio fully into his confidence about the disclosures of the ghost and about his further plan to test Claudius through the performance of a play. When Hamlet reacts to Claudius' breakdown with hysterical glee, he quietly calms him down with a touch of mockery so that they can discuss the implications of Claudius' reaction more sanely.

Hamlet had earlier praised Horatio as one "whose blood and judgment are so well commingled." Upon returning to Denmark, he immediately sends for Horatio as he longs to confide the new horrors of his trip to him and gain his judicial acceptance for his further plans. They meet near a graveyard and, as the sight of skulls being thrown about by the gravedigger leads Hamlet back into morbid reflections on death and decomposition, Horatio again tries to control his friend's excessive sensibility by saying, " 'Twere to consider too curiously, to consider so."

When, after the funeral interruption, they are finally alone again, Hamlet proceeds to explain Claudius' treacherous design upon his life and his own order for the execution of Rosencrantz and Guildenstern. To this Horatio mildly comments, "So Guildenstern and Rosencrantz go to 't." Though Hamlet takes this as an objection and proceeds to excuse his behavior on the grounds of their dangerous complicity with Claudius, whatever objection Horatio might have felt is quickly silenced by Hamlet's aroused reply and he returns to the subject of Hamlet's just grievance against the King. Hamlet now lists his grounds against Claudius and asks for Horatio's judgment as to whether he is not proceeding in "perfect conscience." But Horatio declines to answer this question directly, noting instead the urgency for Hamlet to act immediately if he is to act at all. They are now interrupted by the foppish Osric with his invitation from Claudius for Hamlet's participation in a fencing match with Laertes. During this scene Horatio shows his appreciation for Hamlet's witty undercutting of Osric.

When they are alone again and waiting for the match to begin, Hamlet confides that he feels uneasy about the coming match and Horatio tells him that he should not discount this and should refrain from participating in the match. As he has earlier warned him against following the ghost, so now he does of the fencing match and to as little avail. Hamlet wishes for Horatio's support but he will not abide his restraint. But as Horatio tries to protect Hamlet when he is dying, Hamlet acts to protect his friend from his one passionate gesture, Horatio's desire to follow his friend through suicide. This shows how fully "mortised and adjoined" Horatio feels towards Hamlet. However much he may have questioned Hamlet's reactions and behavior, he has fully committed himself to Hamlet's fate and only permits himself to live so that he may justify Hamlet's life and death. When Hamlet dies he speaks the eulogy over him, commending his "noble heart" and his soul to heaven. With his death, Horatio takes control of events, arranges for the funerals and hands over the kingdom, in accordance with Hamlet's wishes, to Fortinbras.

Throughout the play, Shakespeare has presented Horatio as the norm or model of correct behavior. If there are more things in heaven and earth than are dreamt of in his philosophy, his passionless acceptance of the good and evil in life has resulted in his survival and, with it, the hope for his continuing influence in a healthier state. In Shakespeare's strategy for rehabilitating Hamlet as a proper tragic hero after his descent into evil, Horatio's acceptance of Hamlet's actions during his exile and after his return is most important. And here we come to an important problem in the play. For Horatio's acceptance of Hamlet's murders of Rosencrantz and Guildenstern turn him into as much of a "yes-man" for Hamlet as they were for Claudius, and suggests the cosmic logic for his destruction as well. This may, in fact, be Shakespeare's intention as Hamlet tells Horatio that he should only defer the happiness of death "awhile" until he has told his story.

But the significance of Horatio's acceptance of all of Hamlet's actions and his final eulogy upon him still serves as a vindication for the justice of Hamlet's actions; and here we may convict Shakespeare of "special pleading" for his hero. "Special pleading" occurs when an author so sets the terms of his work that a more positive evaluation for his hero is offered than the objective facts depicted in the work would seem to warrant. The charge of "special pleading" can, moreover, be levelled against the whole *genre* of revenge tragedy from Kyd and Marston to Tourneur. The revenger is a dramatic type of exquisite moral sensibility who is warped by the existence of evil into a being capable of committing with relish more depraved evil than that which he has set out to revenge, but whose character is redeemed at the end and treated heroically. Though Hamlet transcends the type he also represents it and Horatio plays an instrumental role in his perhaps overly favored rehabilitation.

FORTINBRAS   Perhaps the greatest irony in this most ironic of plays is Fortinbras' inheritance of the Danish kingdom. For Fortinbras is the son of the Norwegian King whose defeat was Hamlet's father's greatest victory. If Hamlet's revenge was supposed to vindicate his father's honor, the suicidal way in which he proceeded with this revenge resulted in completely burying his father's glory with his empire. The fifth act began with the clownish gravedigger's commemoration of "that day that our last king Hamlet overcame Fortinbras," and it ends on the day that young Fortinbras inherits the kingdom which was to have come to young Hamlet.

Fortinbras' activities provide a largely unseen backdrop to the play. At the beginning of the first act we learn that Claudius has embarked on massive military preparations to defend Denmark against Fortinbras' martial intentions. Attempting to restore the honor that his father had lost, Fortinbras had levied an army to attack and conquer Denmark. Though son of the late King of Norway, the crown of Norway had gone to his uncle, just as the crown of Denmark had gone to Hamlet's uncle. This shows that in the world of the play it was not unusual for brothers to late kings to be elected to the throne over the pretentions of their younger nephews. But Fortinbras was not prepared to accept his constitutional dispossession so easily. If he had been deprived of the throne of his father, he would try to conquer a kingdom of his own in which, as he later tells Horatio, he has "some rights of memory." Claudius, however, defeats Fortinbras' hopes through diplomatic negotiations with the King of Norway. Informing the old and bedridden King of his nephew's activities and of his allegiance to Denmark, Claudius gets the Norwegian King to curtail Fortinbras' military plans against Denmark.

But Fortinbras is not willing to put an end to his military adventures and so he substitutes for the rich Danish crown a worthless piece of Poland as the object of his plans for conquest. Desiring to win honor through the sword, he cares not that the prize of his glory is worthless or that he will sacrifice thousands of lives and much wealth for this hollow victory. On the passage of this army over Danish soil to Poland, as prearranged with Claudius, Hamlet meets the expedition and comes to admire Fortinbras' heroic resolution to seize honor at all costs. Comparing his own lack of honorable resolution after his father's death with that of Fortinbras, he finds himself deficient and hopes to emulate Fortinbras' endeavors with "bloody" thoughts. Hamlet might well see in Fortinbras a more fitting son to his own father than he has been. Like Hamlet, Sr., Fortinbras is an empire builder who desires only to fight for glory and so, in an ironic way which compounds the irony first mentioned, he is fitted by character to inherit the kingdom of Hamlet, Sr.

Having proven his honor in the successful exploit against Poland, Fortinbras picks the plum of Denmark without any effort. Polonius has earlier said that one can best "by indirections find directions out," and so it has proven to be in the case of Fortinbras. By not attacking Denmark, the Danish crown has fallen into his lap. Here we may again detect the ironic hand of Providence. But what has Providence finally accomplished by its holocaust, its wholesale destruction or sacrifice of the Danish ruling family and its many adjuncts, eight or nine in all? Though ironically defeating Hamlet, Sr.'s glory, it has restored his kingdom to the martial values he had exalted in it, bypassing the secular pacifism of Claudius and the inspired religious dependence of Hamlet. The "mighty opposites" both lie vanquished before the avenging spirit of the ghost whose values are resurrected in Fortinbras and who promises us a restoration to the false values of military honor with its perpetuation of the tragic human condition, of round upon round of excessive glory being punished by the envy it inspires until all are punished by the scourge of heaven.

THE GHOST The mystery of the supernatural background to the action, of that something more within heaven and earth than is dreamt of in most of our secular philosophies, is concentrated in the mysterious figure of the ghost. Whether it be the "honest ghost" of Hamlet's father come from Purgatory or a diabolic or angelic agent of Providence is never made completely clear and this ambiguity reinforces the central mystery of the play. Though Providence accomplishes the destruction of Claudius which the ghost had demanded of Hamlet, his demands also unsettle Hamlet's reason, warp his character and lead to his death as well as the wholesale destruction of the chief members of the court. Such results indicate the morally questionable nature of the ghost's demands and therefore of its nature. Whether it is the true ghost of his father's spirit in Purgatory or a diabolic impersonation of this spirit, the ghost in either case represents an unhallowed spirit and the direct accomplishment of its demands would lead to the damnation of Hamlet. Hamlet's salvation is only assured because he has transcended the ghostly demands for revenge in his final killing of Claudius. But the ghost's influence upon Hamlet has been powerful enough to wrench Hamlet's spirit out of its normal frame so that he destroys himself in the destruction of his enemies.

The ghost appears twice to Hamlet, the first time dressed in the armor which Hamlet, Sr., wore when he won his great victory over Norway and in a setting of military preparations in which his spirit gloried, the second time dressed in his night clothes in the setting of his wife's bedroom. Both scenes represent his most cherished joys and dearest defeats, for his wife betrayed his love through adultery with Claudius and now Claudius is about to negotiate away another glorious victory over Norway followed by the final loss of his empire to the son of the King he had defeated. For these reasons, as well as his murder, the ghost desires the death of Claudius. It wishes Hamlet to quickly dispatch Claudius, take over the kingdom and defeat Fortinbras in battle. Hamlet reveres his father's uncomplicated masculine resolve: " 'A was a man, take him for all in all, / I shall not look upon his life again." But he is himself incapable of such simple heroics. The result is that he destroys himself with the corrupt court and leaves the throne to the inheritance of Fortinbras. Though the ghost's demands do not seem to change in their second interview, its effect upon Hamlet is more "gracious." Hamlet comes to recognize himself as heaven's "scourge and minister" and finally accepts his complete dependence upon the "divinty that shapes our ends." This suggests that the ghost who appears in Gertrude's bedroom is either the more purified spirit of his father or a providential angel who has come to turn Hamlet's spirit from its damnable course and into the way of heaven. Though these identifications can never be made with any certainty, the effect of the ghost's coming is to unleash death and evil onto the stage and to achieve a final scourging of all the past and present evils in the state. If all the victims of avenging Providence fall through flaws in their own characters, the need for such a thorough purgation and the questionable result of Fortinbras' inheritance of the vanquished kingdom remain part of the mysterious "secrets" of supernatural justice which the ghost is forbidden to reveal.

REMAINING SURVIVORS   Of the remaining survivors to the holocaust, the first group may be roughly categorized as courtiers. The most important of these, *Osric*, arrives late on the scene after Claudius' more favored aides have been dispatched either to death or England. In addition to providing some final comic relief before the final scene of destruction, the introduction of Osric is primarily significant for the light it casts on Claudius' spiritual decline. That Claudius, after being freed from the necessity of courting the favors of a fool like Polonius and after gathering to himself such reverential and able courtiers as Rosencrantz and Guildenstern, should be reduced to using such an ostentatious fop as Osric is a sign of his own declining judgment and need for extravagant and uncritical flattery. As Hamlet says of him: "Let a beast be lord of beasts, and his crib shall stand at the king's mess. 'Tis a chough [chatterer], but, as I say, spacious in the possession of dirt." Though Osric may be guilty of criminal complicity in the final plot against Hamlet, he is such a contemptible fool that he is beneath the notice of tragedy. Unlike Polonius, who interfered in his romance with Ophelia, and Rosencrantz and Guildenstern, who betrayed his friendship, Osric has always been too far beneath Hamlet's contempt to betray any trust, and his active association with Hamlet's enemy comes too late to arouse any distracting hatred away from Claudius. Osric's survival, therefore, is partly the product of his complete shallowness and partly of his luck in arriving too late on the scene to capture any sustained attention from Hamlet.

Of the others, *Voltemand* and *Cornelius* serve only as Claudius' ambassadors of peace to Norway, and this solitary and good service frees them from any association with the guilt of Claudius. With Horatio, they represent the positive elements in the court with which Fortinbras may build a better society. There is also a *Gentleman* who appears twice in association with Horatio, once when they go to prevail upon Gertrude to see Ophelia and the other time when he brings Horatio the sailor with his letters from Hamlet. His compassion seems also to bode well for Denmark. Of the many other unnamed *Lords, Ladies, Messengers* and *Attendants* who people the stage, the most important are the *English Ambassadors,* for they serve to report the deaths of Rosencrantz and Guildenstern and their entrance serves as the knock of fate which closes the "interim" during which Hamlet's revenge must needs have been completed. The other Lords and Ladies serve as the background of any state. They believe, with Rosencrantz and Guildenstern, in the divine right of kings, and all cry "Treason! treason!" when Claudius is wounded by Hamlet. If Fortinbras does not make use of such willing tools of villainy as Osric and *Reynaldo,* Polonius' well instructed servant, Denmark's hopes are good; but such willing tools are, unfortunately, always available, and the remainder of the court will support even a corrupt king.

In addition to the courtiers, the state also makes use of a "churlish" *Priest.* As he is referred to in the stage directions as a Doctor of Divinity, the suggestion is that he is a Protestant. In any case, he represents the forces of established religion with its preference for the letter over the spirit of the law. Because Ophelia's death was "doubtful," he does not permit her the full pomp of a religious funeral. For this Laertes suggests that "A minist'ring angel shall my sister be / When thou liest howling."

To the representatives of court and church we must now add the army. Despite the bloody honor of its royal leaders, this group represents one of the most healthy elements in the state and stands in marked contrast to the courtiers. *Francisco* we just see for a fleeting moment before he is relieved at his sentry duty by *Bernardo,* who is soon after joined by his more important fellow officer, *Marcellus.* Both Bernardo and Marcellus are honest men with a healthy religious dread and a superstitious awe of ghosts. Marcellus has brought Horatio along for his opinion on the ghost and himself offers the belief that ghosts and other supernatural phenomena are opposed by the religion of Christ. He later offers the most pregnant remark on the significance of the ghost's coming, that "something is rotten in the state of Denmark." With a natural sense of honor combined with his religious dread, he does not wish to "swear" to confirm his already given word to his secrecy. It is perhaps the incorruptible integrity of the common Danish soldier which has led Claudius to surround himself with "Switzers," mercenary Swiss guards such as to this day protect the Vatican. But what is true of the Danish soldiers is also true of their Norwegian counterparts. On his trip to the sea, Hamlet meets a *Captain* of the Norwegian army who is just as blunt and honest a fellow as Bernardo and Marcellus. Completely unimpressed by Fortinbras' mission against Poland, he criticizes this futile pursuit of honor with the homely words: "We go to gain a little patch of ground / That hath in it no profit but the name. / To pay five ducats, five, I should not farm it." With as natural a religious feeling as the Danish soldiers, he bids farewell to Hamlet with the words, "God bye you, sir."

In addition to the various soldiers, Hamlet maintains an easy familiarity with other uncourtly members of society. For the *Players* he has a special affection and tells Polonius that they should "be well used, for they are the abstract and brief chronicles of the time." When Polonius replies that he will "use them according to their desert," Hamlet returns with natural Christian charity, "God's bodkin, man, much better! Use every man after his desert, and who shall scape whipping?" He joins in with them in dramatic recitation and works familiarly with them on the play they are to perform.

Of other rogues and peasant slaves, there are two groups with whom Hamlet enters into easy friendship. The first are the pirates who attack the Danish ship taking Hamlet to England and who capture Hamlet. Of them Hamlet says, "they have dealt with me like thieves of mercy," and he further refers to them as "good fellows." Of these *Sailors* who come to Horatio with Hamlet's letter, one of them greets Horatio with the words, "God bless you, sir." When Horatio replies, "Let him bless thee too," the sailor returns with easy confidence in the disposition of Providence, " 'A shall, sir, an't please him." The second group are the clowns who play the part of *Gravediggers*. With a Christian sense of democracy, the chief Gravedigger says: "And the more pity that great folk should have count'nance in this world to drown or hang themselves more than their even-Christen. Come, my spade. There is no ancient gentlemen but gard'ners, ditchers, and grave-makers. They hold up Adam's profession." Singing casually of the loss of youth and the sweetness of young love with the coming of age and final death, "custom," says Horatio, has made the fact of death "in him a property of easiness." As familiar with skulls as he is with Hamlet, he reflects with relish on the pleasure of life one of these grinning skulls once gave him when the man was alive: "A pestilence on him for a mad rogue! 'A poured a flagon of Rhenish on my head once. This same skull, sir, was—sir—Yorick's skull, the king's jester." Rogues and peasants these jesters and clowns, players, pirates, soldiers and gravediggers may be, but they are the salt of the earth. They are "even-Christen" with all men of goodwill, and their easy endurance in the face of death and easy familiarity with their Maker is the hope of their world. Hamlet may have transcended their religious understanding in a profound perception of divinity, but he can still be "even-Christen" with them. Though Fortinbras has inherited the world of the court and will perpetuate its false sense of honor, however purified of its grosser abuses, these nameless "good fellows" are Hamlet's legacy and they endure through all dynastic changes. It is ironically to Hamlet's final credit that he can claim: "O, what a rogue and peasant slave am I!"

COMMENTARY ON THE CRITICISM OF *HAMLET*

One of the first critical comments on *Hamlet* might serve as an apt reminder to all of the later critics who, with such infinite variety, have agreed only to disagree. In his *Discourse upon Comedy* written in 1702, the major comic playwright George Farquhar referred to *Hamlet* as "long the Darling of the English Audience, and like to continue with the same Applause, in Defiance of all the Criticism that were ever publish'd in Greek, and Latin."

QUESTIONS ABOUT KEY POINTS IN THE CRITICISM   In the course of the past few hundred years, the major critics of *Hamlet* have raised certain central questions about the play.

1.   A primary question is whether this celebrated tragedy is a perfect work of art.

2.   The most consistently raised question concerns the nature of Hamlet. Is he a healthy Renaissance prince, a depraved egomaniac, or an essentially noble and sensitive hero whose spirit has been disturbed by the task of revenge imposed upon him. If the latter is true, what has so disturbed him as to seriously delay the prosecution of his revenge? Is it a weak will, the product of over-intellectualizing, the result of melancholy, or an Oedipus Complex?

3.   The third and most recently raised question concerns the relative importance of Hamlet's character to the structure of the play as a whole. Does the mystery of Hamlet's disturbance point to a deeper mystery at the heart of the play? Is this mystery a fault or a virtue of the design? What is the relationship of the ghost to this mystery? Is *Hamlet* finally to be understood as a religious drama? These and their related questions will be discussed in the following historical survey of the outstanding criticism on *Hamlet*.

DR. JOHNSON'S CRITICISM   The first major critical treatment of *Hamlet* is that of Dr. Samuel Johnson in the various notes on the play that he wrote in 1765. His is probably the first partially negative criticism on the play and its leading character, and the major lines of his criticism have continued to be reflected in later trends of criticism. Dr. Johnson criticizes Shakespeare's workmanship on two major counts: inadequate motivation for Hamlet's feigned madness ("for he does nothing which he might not have done with the reputation of sanity") and a faulty catastrophe.

HAMLET VIEWED AS AN ARTISTIC FAILURE In more recent
times this approach has been taken in J.M. Robertson's *The Problem
of Hamlet,* E.E. Stoll's *Hamlet, an Historical and Comparative
Study,* and T.S. Eliot's "Hamlet and His Problems," all appearing
in 1919. Eliot has accepted and popularized the position of Robertson and Stoll that the play represents an imperfect fusion of old
crude material with new with the result that, in Eliot's words, "the
play is most certainly an artistic failure." Robertson's conclusion is
that Shakespeare shifted the emphasis of his play to Hamlet's
"tortures on the score of his mother's degradation" and then was
unable to fuse this new motive with the "intractable" material from
the old play. Eliot continues: "Hamlet (the man) is dominated
by an emotion which is inexpressible, because it is in *excess* of
the facts as they appear. . . . We should have to understand things
which Shakespeare did not understand himself." The bafflement of
critics through the ages as to the cause of Hamlet's delay and the
nature of his psychological problem is seen to result from "the
bafflement of his creator in the face of his artistic problem." Ernest
Jones' more recent attempt to explain that "which Shakespeare did
not understand himself" will be dealt with more fully later in this
discussion. For the moment it is important to point out that if
Jones is right that the solution to the problem of Hamlet is that he
had an "Oedipus Complex" of which Shakespeare could not have
been consciously aware, then we are left with the conclusion
that Shakespeare worked with emotional materials in the play
which he understood and portrayed imperfectly and that the play,
therefore, is seriously flawed at its heart. We shall later see that
what Eliot and his predecessors regarded as an artistic flaw has
come to be regarded by a later school of critics as a prime artistic
virtue of the play. But the point which Eliot's group makes must
not be dsimissed too lightly; for, whether by design or not, it may
well be that the difficulty most critics have encountered with *Hamlet*
is due to the core of unexplained mystery at the heart of the play.

HAMLET'S CHARACTER VIEWED AS EVIL The second objection Dr. Johnson makes is to the moral nature of Hamlet. He
noted that Hamlet treats Ophelia with "wanton cruelty" and that
the speech made over the praying figure of Claudius "in which
Hamlet, represented as a virtuous character, is not content with
taking blood for blood, but contrives damnation for the man that
he would punish, is too horrible to be read or to be uttered." In
more recent times this objection has been elaborated by such critics
as G. Wilson Kgnht and Salvador de Madariaga. In "The Embassy
of Death: An Essay on Hamlet," published in 1930 in the volume
entitled *The Wheel of Fire,* Knight argues for "a striking reversal
of the usual commentary," namely that Claudius represents the
human instincts, Hamlet the inhuman. He argues as follows:
"Hamlet is inhuman. He has seen through humanity. And this

inhuman cynicism, however justifiable in this case, on the plane
of causality and individual responsibility, is a deadly and venomous
thing. Instinctively the creatures of earth—Laertes, Polonius,
Ophelia, Rosencrantz and Guildenstern, league themselves with
Claudius: they are of his kind. . . . But Hamlet is not of flesh and
blood, he is a spirit of penetrating intellect and cynicism and
misery, without faith in himself or any one else, murdering his love
of Ophelia, on the brink of insanity, taking delight in cruelty, tor-
turing Claudius, wringing his mother's heart, a poison in the midst
of the healthy bustle of the court. He is a superman among men.
And he is a superman because he has walked and held converse
with Death, and his consciousness works in terms of Death and
the Negation of Cynicism. . . . Thus Hamlet is an element of evil
in the state of Denmark. . . . Not till it has slain all, is the demon
that grips Hamlet satisfied. And last it slays Hamlet himself: 'The
spirit that I have seen / May be the devil. . . .' It was." Hamlet
is seen as an inhuman evil compelled by the devil, who has im-
personated his father's ghost, to spread its poison throughout the
state of Denmark until all are destroyed. Madariaga's book, On
Hamlet, published in 1948, reflects in yet more elaborated form
this view of Hamlet as a brutal egotist, indifferent to other human
beings. Though such a view as the total interpretation of Hamlet
must surely be considered extreme in the light of Shakespeare's
positive treatment of his hero through much of the play, there is
enough evidence in support of it to make any interpretation which
totally discounts it as much in error. Hamlet's moral decline at
the moments pointed to by Dr. Johnson can hardly be denied, and
if they do not add up to a total portrait of egomania and inhuman
evil, any interpretation which aims at completeness must make some
allowance for some such traits of character at least at some points
in the action.

GREBANIER'S ARGUMENT FOR A "HEALTHY" HAMLET
There has been, nonetheless, an insistent line of criticism stretching
from Joseph Ritson in 1783 to Bernard Grebanier in 1960 that
Hamlet did not procrastinate, was not unduly disturbed, and went
about his revenge as efficiently as circumstances permitted. In The
Heart of Hamlet, Grebanier makes the most extended argument
for a "healthy" Hamlet: "To know how Hamlet feels about life
we must watch not what he says about it so much as what he does
living it. Look at him in this way, and you will find him not melancholy, not complex-ridden, not pessimistic, not even disillusioned
basically—but a healthy, vigorous man, much in love with life,
who, given the slightest opportunity, is happy, cheerful, companion-
able, and kind." Grebanier defeats his own argument, of course,
by the condition he makes that we must disregard everything
Hamlet says to the contrary—which makes up the majority of his
speeches. The same is true for his outline of the action: "As the

second act concludes, there is still no question of procrastination. Hamlet has seized the very first oportunity that has presented itself for procuring answers to some fundamental questions. . . . Also, there has been no occasion for his feigning madness." Grebanier destroys his position in the very next line of his exposition (p. 170): "The next day. Guildenstern and Rosencrantz admit to the King and Queen that they have failed to determine the cause of Hamlet's distraction." Though Grebanier fails to see any evidence of Hamlet's madness, feigned or real, it is clear from his own description of the play that Claudius does and is worried by it. It is impossible, therefore, to accept Grebanier's conclusion: "Shakespeare's Hamlet, then, is not a play about a man who procrastinates or a man who feigns madness. Neither appears in the work." But if Grebanier's theory of a "healthy" Hamlet represents one of the most serious as well as influential misreadings of the play in modern times, it does serve to focus attention upon Hamlet's remarkable amount of activity and upon his rashness: "Hamlet falls not because he is too timid, too sensitive, too thoughtful, or too scrupulous, but because he is too rash, too overweening, too heedless." It is unfortunate, however, that in an interpretation based largely on Hamlet's rashness, Grebanier also ignores what Hamlet has to say about this and so misses the whole theological context in which Hamlet places his rash activity.

GOETHE'S INTERPRETATION OF HAMLET AS NOBLY WEAK-WILLED Between these two extremes of Hamlet's total diseased depravity or total moral and psychological health lies the major bulk of criticism on the play. This major historical tradition accepts Hamlet as an example of Aristotle's model tragic hero, one who is generally better than the average but is brought down by flaw in his character. The first major proponent of this position was Johann Wolfgang von Goethe in his *Wilhelm Meister's Apprenticeship,* written in 1796: "Shakespeare sought to depict a great deed laid upon a soul unequal to the performance of it. . . . A beautiful, pure, noble and most moral nature, without the strength of nerve which forms a hero, sinks beneath a burden which it can neither bear nor throw off; every duty is holy to him—this is too hard. The impossible is required of him—not the impossible in itself, but the impossible to him. How he winds, turns, agonizes, advances, and recoils, ever reminded, ever reminding himself, and at last almost loses his purpose from his thoughts, without ever again recovering his peace of mind." Goethe's noble but weak-willed hero has had long critical and theatrical popularity. It is to be regretted that his other insight into the play has been less observed: "the hero has no plan . . . but the piece is full of plan . . . as it is Fate that draws the plan . . . the work is tragic in its highest sense, and admits of no other than a tragic end." Dr. Johnson has also noted that "Hamlet is, through the whole play, rather an instrument than an agent." But neither Johnson nor Goethe connect Hamlet's passivity and the active shaping of Fate through the structure of the play with Hamlet's perception of the shaping role of Fate or Divinity in human destiny.

COLERIDGE'S INTERPRETATION OF HAMLET AS OVER-IN-TELLECTUAL This last point the next great interpreter of *Hamlet,* Samuel Taylor Coleridge, did partially perceive in *Lecture* XII (Collier Report) of the 1811-12 series: "He [Shakespeare] saw at once how consistent it was with the character of Hamlet, that after still resolving, and still deferring, still determining to execute, and still postponing the execution, he should finally, in the infirmity of his disposition, give himself up to his destiny, and hopelessly place himself in the power, and at the mercy of his enemies." Coleridge's interpretation of Hamlet largely derives from that of Goethe, as we can see in the following comment: "Such a mind as Hamlet's is near akin to madness . . . that greatness of genius, which led Hamlet to a perfect knowledge of his own character, which, with all strength of motive, was so weak as to be unable to carry into act his own most obvious duty." But he disagrees with Johnson's horror at Hamlet's character: "The fact, however, is that Dr. Johnson did not understand the character of Hamlet, and censured accordingly: the determination to allow the guilty King to escape at such a moment is only part of the indecision and irresoluteness of the hero. Hamlet seizes hold of a pretext for not acting, when he might have acted so instantly and effectually. . . ." While we may agree with Coleridge that Hamlet was rationalizing a cause for delay, we may, however, also share Dr. Johnson's horror at the form Hamlet's rationalization took. Coleridge, however, saw Hamlet's weakness as resulting wholly from an over-intellectual cast of mind. He had elaborated this position as early as 1808 in his notes for another lecture: "In Hamlet I conceive him [Shakespeare] to have wished to exemplify the moral necessity of a due balance between our attention to outward objects and our meditation on inward thoughts—a due balance between the real and the imaginary world. In Hamlet this balance does not exist—his thoughts, images, and fancy [being] far more vivid than his perceptions, and his perceptions instantly passing thro' the medium of his contemplations, and acquiring as they pass a form and color not naturally their own. Hence great, enormous, intellectual activity, and a consequent aversion to real action, with all its symptoms and accompanying qualities."

BRADLEY'S INTERPRETATION OF HAMLET AS PATHOLOGI-CALLY MELANCHOLIC By the end of the nineteenth century, the Goethe-Coleridge interpretation of Hamlet as nobly weak-willed and over-intellectual had become standard. A.C. Bradley's important essay on Hamlet in *Shakespearean Tragedy,* written in

1904, represents both the critique and culmination of romantic criticism. Bradley's key to Hamlet's character is a pathological state of melancholy. In his discussion of this he also provides a critique of Coleridge's reigning theory: "The direct cause [of Hamlet's delay] was a state of mind quite abnormal and induced by special circumstances, ["the moral shock of the sudden ghastly disclosure of his mother's true nature"]—a state of profound melancholy. Now, Hamlet's reflectiveness doubtless played a certain part in the *production* of that melancholy, and was thus one indirect contributory cause of his irresolution. And, again, the melancholy, once established, displayed, as one of its symptoms, an excessive reflection on the required deed. But excess of reflection was not, as the theory makes it, the *direct* cause of the irresolution at all . . . it is to be considered rather a symptom of his state than a cause of it . . . it is downright impossible that the man we see rushing after the Ghost, killing Polonius, dealing with the King's commission on the ship, boarding the pirate, leaping into the grave, executing his final vengeance, could *ever* have been shrinking or slow in an emergency. Imagine Coleridge doing any of these things!" Long before Grebanier, Bradley pointed out Hamlet's high level of activity but not at the expense of supposing him thereby healthy. For Bradley shows that melancholy "accounts for Hamlet's energy as well as for his lassitude." He also attributes to Hamlet's melancholy those "painful features of his character" which Johnson had first noted and which Knight and Madariaga were later to elaborate as the whole of Hamlet's character: "his almost savage irritability on the one hand, and on the other his self-absorption, his callousness, his insensibility to the fates of those whom he despises, and to the feelings even of those whom he loves." But Bradley judges Hamlet's basic and original character as being "by temperament . . . inclined to nervous instability," as having both "an exquisite sensibility, to which we may give the name 'moral,' and "intellectual genius." As such, he feels that *Hamlet* deserves the title 'tragedy of moral idealism' . . ." Bradley is, therefore, in the line of criticism which has extended from Goethe through Coleridge. And though he considers the psychological impediment greater than the intellectual, he also feels that it is Hamlet's genius which raises his story from the pathological to the tragic and makes Hamlet "the symbol of a tragic mystery inherent in human nature."

JONES' PSYCHOANALYTIC INTERPRETATION OF HAMLET AS HAVING AN OEDIPUS COMPLEX From the perspective of the untrained psychologist, Bradley's interpretation must remain the soundest and most complete interpretation of Hamlet's unquestionably disturbed personality. It has the further advantage of working within the psychological terms familiar to Shakespeare

and his contemporaries. But in this day of psychoanalysis it is not surprising that we should have been offered a specialist's analysis of Hamlet's disorder by the eminently qualified Ernest Jones, student and biographer of Freud. First developed in 1923 in his *Essays in Applied Psycho-Analysis* and later elaborated in the book length *Hamlet and Oedipus* of 1949, Jones has presented the definitive psychoanalytic interpretation of Hamlet. In a well-reasoned analysis that shows full knowledge of the critical traditions and of the play, Jones argues "that Hamlet's hesitancy was due to some special cause of repugnance for his task and that he was unaware of the nature of this repugnance." Jones then shows that the source of this repugnance stems from the activation of his repressed childhood Oedipus Complex: "The actual realization of his early wish in the death of his father at the hands of a jealous rival would then have stimulated into activity these 'repressed' memories, [that he had "secretly wished him out of the way so that he might enjoy undisputed and undisturbed the monopoly of" his mother's affection], which would have produced, in the form of depression and other suffering, an obscure aftermath of his childhood's conflict. . . . The explanation, therefore, of the delay and self-frustration exhibited in the endeavor to fulfill his father's demand for vengeance is that to Hamlet the thought of incest and parricide combined is too intolerable to be borne." This leads to behavior which today "is given the name of psychoneurosis, and long ago the genius of Shakespeare depicted it for us with faultless insight."

OBJECTIONS TO JONES' INTERPRETATION   While Jones had illuminated recesses in the psychology of Hamlet that have been considered hopelessly mysterious by Hamlet and most of the critics of his personality who followed him, there are two objections to this interpretation being considered more than a most fascinating but finally irrelevant account. The first of these is that as it could not have been part of Shakespeare's design, it is irrelevant to the artistic meaning of the work. The second is the objection that Bradley raised even to his more historically acceptable psychological account, that "the psychological point of view is not equivalent to the tragic." It is not the hidden psychological impediment which makes a tragic hero of Hamlet but the way in which his genius works to cope with and finally transcend this impediment. Jones concludes: "This is at all events the mechanism that is actually found in the real Hamlets who are investigated psychologically." But the difference between the "real Hamlets" who lie on the couches of today's psychoanalysts and Shakespeare's Hamlet is that the created character transcends his "insoluble inner conflict" in a profound and, from the point of view of the play, valid religious commitment.

WILSON AND THE NEW DIRECTIONS IN CRITICISM   The burden of most critical comment on the play in the past three hundred years has been the attempt to explain Hamlet's psychology. It seems unlikely that future criticism will improve upon Bradley's interpretation as footnoted by Jones' persuasive psychoanalysis. But the very excellence of Bradley's interpretation coupled with his own objection as to the final adequacy of a single focus upon Hamlet's psychology has led to new directions in criticism. This has largely been a shift of emphasis from Hamlet's psychology to the structure and meaning of the play itself. One of the first attempts in this direction was the effort of Robertson and Stoll to compare the play with its antecedents. This led to the extreme view that the play was a partial artistic failure. Most other attempts, however, have resulted in more positive conclusions. The most important of these is probably John Dover Wilson's *What Happens in Hamlet,* 1935. Wilson's primary concern is to make sense of the plot, and this he does, though sometimes he does so in an overly ingenious way. In this last category may be included his suggestions that Hamlet overheard the plot to test him with Ophelia and that Claudius did not notice the dumb show because he was busy discussing Hamlet's attentions to Ophelia with Polonius. More important, perhaps, is his extended treatment of the significance of the ghost, giving historical background on the Renaissance attitude towards ghosts and suggesting the permanent ambiguity of Shakespeare's presentation. He also focuses our attention on the multiple investigations which take up most of the action in the second and third acts. The mystery first suggested by the ghost and later accentuated through the cross investigations of Hamlet, Claudius and Polonius is finally seen to extend to the character of Hamlet, himself: "In fine, we were never intended to reach the heart of the mystery. That it has a heart is an illusion; the mystery itself is an illusion; Hamlet is an illusion. The secret that lies behind it all is not Hamlet's, but Shakespeare's: the technical devices he employed to create this supreme illusion of a great and mysterious character. . . ." In seeing the sense of mystery as product of the consummate design of Shakespeare rather than as an artistic flaw, Wilson has set the line for much of the criticism which has followed.

THE COSMIC MYSTERY OF *HAMLET*   In 1942, the influential critic C.S. Lewis followed Wilson's footsteps in his essay, "Hamlet: The Prince or the Poem?" Continuing the shift of emphasis from the prince to the poem, he concludes: "Their error, in my view, was to put the mystery in the wrong place—in Hamlet's motives rather than in that darkness which enwraps Hamlet and the whole tragedy and all who read or watch it. It is a mysterious play in the sense of being a play about mystery." Little is added to this line of criticism in Maynard Mack's essay of 1952, "The World of *Hamlet*," which follows Caroline Spurgeon's earlier (1935) lead in imagery analysis to point finally at the "mysterious" quality of Hamlet's world. It was finally for the Greek scholar H.D.F. Kitto to draw the growing conclusion in his book of 1956, *Form and Meaning in Drama:* "What if *Hamlet* is a play which it would be reasonable to call 'religious drama,' as we are using the term here? What if the ingrained individualism of the last two centuries—-to say nothing of romanticism—has blinded us to one aspect of the play without which it cannot possibly appear as a firm and coherent structure? . . . the architectonic pattern just indicated is so vast as to suggest at once that what we are dealing with is no individual tragedy of character, however profound, but something more like religious drama. . . . The conception which unites these eight persons in one coherent catastrophe may be said to be this: evil, once started on its course, will so work as to attack and overthrow impartially the good and the bad; and if the dramatist makes us feel, as he does, that a Providence is ordinant in all this, that, as with the Greeks, is his way of universalizing the particular event." It is not only we, however, but also Hamlet who comes to understand this. In G.R. Elliott's very detailed treatment of the play in 1951, *Scourge and Minister: a Study of Hamlet as Tragedy of Revengefulness and Justice,* Hamlet's downward and then upward development is carefully traced, though with some over-simplification, with the final conclusion: "Thus Hamlet, in sharp contrast with his state of mind in the central scenes of the drama . . . has finally come to terms with his conscience and with Providence . . . because he believes he sees, in and through and above all, 'heaven ordinant.' " Thus the most recent criticism of *Hamlet* has come to see Hamlet's character as involved with a larger Providential design which works through him and the other characters and with which Hamlet's spirit finally comes to terms. If the play points to a question, as Harry Levin suggests in his 1959 book, *The Question of Hamlet,* the question is related to the final religious mystery of existence.

SAMPLE ESSAY QUESTIONS AND ANSWERS

Q. 1: Does Hamlet procrastinate in prosecuting his revenge?

A. 1: Despite recent arguments, particularly by Grebanier, to the effect that Hamlet does not procrastinate because he has moral scruples about the validity of the ghost's evidence until after Claudius' guilty response to the performance of the play within the play and then only has a single opportunity before his exile which he does not utilize because he finds Claudius' praying and prefers to wait until he can catch him in an act which has "no relish of salvation in't," the answer would seem to be an emphatic yes, in accordance with a long tradition of criticism. Though the dramatic action of the play does not reveal more than the single opportunity when Claudius is alone in prayer, this dramatised opportunity occurs two months after the meeting with the ghost when Hamlet had said that he would be "swift" and "sweep to my revenge." In the "rogue and peasant slave" soliloquy, which occurs shortly before the so-called "single opportunity," Hamlet admits that he has been "unpregnant of my cause" and wonders whether he is a "coward." It is only after he is filled with disgust with himself for his long delay that he rationalizes his delay with an admittedly sound scruple about the evidence of the ghost and decides to test it by performing a dramatized repetition of Claudius' crime before his eyes. When he has his opportunity shortly after confirming Claudius' guilt, he rationalizes it away with the damnable argument that Claudius' soul might escape eternal damnation. But that this was not his single opportunity is shown shortly after, when, *en route* to his exile in England, Hamlet refers to his "dull revenge" in the important soliloquy in which he admits: "I do not know / Why yet I live to say 'This thing's to do'; / Sith I have cause and will and strength and means / To do't." And he now vows, in opposition to his attitude of the past two months: "O! from this time forth, / My thoughts be bloody, or be nothing worth!"

Q. 2: If Hamlet does procrastinate, what is the reason for his delay?

A. 2: We have now come to the "problem of Hamlet," for which there are as many solutions as critics. Goethe believed that Hamlet's soul, though pure and noble, had insufficient strength of nerve to perform the task imposed upon it. In opposition to this interpretation, it may be argued that Hamlet's soul was not quite so "pure" since, as Dr. Johnson first pointed out, the reason Hamlet gives for not murdering Claudius during his prayers "is too horrible to be read or to be uttered." As for the weakness of his nerve, the speed and lack of guilt with which he is able to dispatch Polonius, Rosencrantz and Guildenstern, not to speak of the way he boards the pirate ship in the midst of battle, would seem to argue against this view.

The second important interpretation is that of Coleridge who believed that Hamlet's overly intellectual cast of mind inhibited him from taking any decisive action. Hamlet, himself, gives some support to this view in two of his soliloques. In the "to be or not to be" soliloquy which, with its balanced list of alternatives, is a perfect exercise in intellectual reasoning, Hamlet concludes: "Thus conscience [consciousness] does make cowards of us all; / And thus the native hue of resolution / Is sicklied o'er with the pale cast of thought." Again, in the soliloquy *en route* to exile, Hamlet wonders whether the delay in his revenge is due to "some craven scruple / Of thinking too precisely on the event, / A thought, which, quarter'd, hath but one part wisdom, and ever three parts coward." While there is no question that Hamlet has a brilliant intellectual mind and devotes much time to thinking about his problems, the starting point of his tortured musings is never the reasons his mind offers for not taking action but the very unexplained fact of his delay, a fact which his mind then proceeds in a most brilliant fashion to attempt to rationalize away. Thus, having considered the hypothesis that his delay is due to "thinking too precisely on the event," he immediately continues, "I do not know / why yet I live to say 'This thing's to do," thereby completely rejecting this possible explanation.

The psychological explanation of Bradley, based on the psychological theories of Shakespeare's time, that Hamlet was in a pathological state of melancholy seems closer to the point. This melancholy, induced by the ghost's "disclosure of his mother's true nature" though, we might add, that it probably originated earlier in the shock produced by his father's death and mother's remarriage, as Gertrude, herself, suggests, accounts, according to Bradley, "for his energy as well as his lassitude," for his "savage irritability" and "self-absorption." As Hamlet explains to Rosencrantz and Guildenstern: "I have of late,—but wherefore I know not,—lost all my mirth, forgone all custom of exercises; and indeed it goes so heavily with my disposition that this goodly frame, the earth, seems to me a sterile promontory." Hamlet here admits that he is in a state of melancholy though he cannot fathom its source. In this state of melancholy, he cannot bring himself to concentrate on any concerted plan of action. Thus, in the exile soliliquy, the first possibility he suggests for his "dull revenge" is "bestial oblivion," simply forgetting about the task of revenge for long periods of melancholic self-absorption until some chance event pricks his conscience and starts his brain working to provide a rationalized excuse and forced resolution which brings him no closer to the accomplishment of his task.

More recently, the psychoanalyst Ernest Jones has attempted to explain the ultimate source of Hamlet's melancholy, that source which neither Hamlet nor Shakespeare was able to fathom. In strictly Freudian terms, Jones suggests that Hamlet had an Oedipus Complex, that Claudius' accomplishment of Hamlet's own repressed desire to murder his father and marry his mother had caused Hamlet to identify himself subconsciously with Claudius so that any thought of murdering Claudius tended to reactivate his repressed desires with the result that he tried to evade these painful subconscious associations in "bestial oblivion." Furthermore, the subconscious identification with Claudius also meant that Claudius' death for these sins also implied his own death, which made the planning of revenge still more difficult. While this analysis is most interesting, its primary difficulty lies in the very fact that it explains everything on a sub-conscious level which has no real existence in the play.

Though it would appear that Hamlet has some psychological impediment to the performance of the particular task of revenging his father's murder, its ultimate source is not disclosed in the play. Robertson, Stoll and Eliot have considered this lack of sufficient explanation to be an artistic failure of the play, but Wilson concludes that it is a purposeful mystery, part of the pattern of mystery which underlines the whole play. The final answer, if answer it be, would seem to be that provided by Hamlet, himself—"I do not know."

Q. 3:   In what sense is Hamlet the hero and Claudius the villain of the play?

A. 3:   The answer to this is hardly as simple as it was long held to be, for, in terms of murder, Hamlet stands as guilty as Claudius. Although Claudius had committed adultery with his brother's wife and then killed him to gain his crown and the freedom to marry Gertrude, when we first see him, he appears to be an able administrator of the state, concerned to preserve peace through negotiation rather than rush into wholesale war. Furthermore, he has an essentially moral nature which can be moved to experience such guilt that it leads him into religious despair. Where Claudius at first appears to represent the corrupt though life-affirming aspect of the play, Hamlet's original purity of soul is so sickened by the evil in the world that he has experienced, suspected and under-covered that he becomes a spirit of negation, moved in alternation by the impulse to suicide and murder. Though the ghost's reve-lations serve to channel his hostility and to sanction it as a refor-mation of the evils in society, they also aggravate his already dis-turbed psychological state and so warp his character that, as he tells Gertrude, he "must be cruel only to be kind." In this con-dition, he rejects the possibility of killing a contrite Claudius be-cause his soul might escape eternal damnation, mercilessly taunts and unknowingly kills Polonius only to still further insult his lifeless corpse, treats Ophelia with such cruelty that it contributes to her loss of sanity and final death, and first taunts and then arranges for the executions of Rosencrantz and Guildenstern with-out permitting them time for confession and absolution. In fact, at the moment when Claudius kneels contritely in prayer and Hamlet stands over him with sword drawn and the evil desire not only to destroy his body but also to damn his soul, it would seem that it is Claudius who is the hero and Hamlet the villain.

But if Hamlet has savagely lashed out with tongue and hand in all directions even though procrastinating in his purposed revenge while Claudius has wished only to be left alone to enjoy the fruits of his one crime, restraining himself with enormous patience and control from ridding himself of the maddening presence of Hamlet until Hamlet's murder of Polonius convinces Claudius of his own personal danger, it is still Claudius who is the true villain and Hamlet the hero in the spiritual world of Shakespeare's play. For, to Shakespeare, that which distinguishes the hero from the villain is the perception of man's necessary dependence on the divine will. Though Claudius had counseled Hamlet that his refusal to accept the death of his father "shows a will most incorrect to heaven," he had himself been guilty of the same inability to accept the divine dispensation that gave his brother the crown and woman he loved and had plotted to shape his own destiny by first murdering his brother and then planning the death of Hamlet who alone stood in the way of his enjoyment of the fruits of his original crime. He had made himself the god of his own universe and when all his attempts to shape his ends backfire, he dies in a condition of self-delusion and spiritual unreadiness.

Hamlet also begins in a state of spiritual alienation from God's purposes, unable to accept God's creation while prevented by His law from committing suicide. But after murdering Polonius in a moment of temporary insanity, he suddenly understands his re-lationship to the divine in a new light: "heaven hath pleas'd it so, / To punish me with this, and this with me, / That I must be their scourge and minister." He had acted while beside himself and the fact that this unknowing action succeeded in ridding the court of one of its prime sources of corruption he takes to be the result of divine prompting. That he shall also be punished for his heavenly prompted scourging, he accepts as a necessary contingency of his new ministry. Where before he had felt alienated from the divine will, he now feels himself to be in harmony with it and sees himself as a vessel for the fulfillment of Providence. This new insight becomes even more deeply perceived after another rash act while on ship bound for England, an act which seals the fate of his old school fellows Rosencrantz and Guildenstern. In a most important speech in which he praises his rashness, he explains:

> And praised be rashness for it—let us know,
> Our indiscretion sometimes serves us well
> When our deep plots do pall, and that should learn us
> There's a divinity that shapes our ends,
> Rough-hew them how we will—

He returns to Denmark convinced that Providence will arrange the means by which he may destroy the cancer in his country, Claudius, who, not content with killing his brother and King while committing adultery with his brother's wife and then assuming the throne that Hamlet had hoped would come to himself, now has planned by the most underhanded means to destroy Hamlet's own life. It is not now to revenge his father's murder on the basis of dubious spectral evidence that he purposes but a judicial execution for planning his own death, for which he now had written evidence. Though he knows he only has time to accomplish his purpose until the English Ambassadors return with the news of the deaths of Rosencrantz and Guildenstern, he is convinced that "the interim is mine."

And so it proves. Although Hamlet had returned without taking any precautions for his safety or making any plans for the death of Claudius, the duel with Laertes, in which both Hamlet and Laertes are mortally wounded and the Queen poisoned, due to the backfiring of Claudius' "deep plots," leads to Laertes' confession before the assembled court of Claudius' guilt which, in turn, permits Hamlet to execute Claudius judicially. Though he is himself mortally punished for his divine ministry, he has not finally taken a possibly damnable personal revenge but has been enabled to perform the divine will through his complete dependence upon Providence. He dies believing that "the readiness is all," having finally achieved the ability to accept both life and death and his last acts, the restraining of Horatio from suicide and his voting Fortinbras the new King, are his most life-affirming. Where Claudius is unready for death and has damned himself by the piling up of evil plots to shape his ends, Hamlet has most nobly won his salvation.

Q. 4:   How do the minor characters function to enhance Hamlet's
moral stature?

A. 4:   We have already seen how Claudius, whom Hamlet calls
his "mighty opposite," serves as a moral contrast to Hamlet, but the
minor characters also serve as foils to illuminate Hamlet's true
worth, a necessary procedure since Shakespeare has omitted no
pains in painting Hamlet's evil propensities and thus has risked
alienating the audience's sympathies from his hero. The first of
these foil characters is Ophelia who is placed in a spiritual situation
which parallels that in which we first encounter Hamlet. The mysterious death of her father and, as it seems to her, the cruel betrayal
by her lover lead to the loss of her sanity and the probable taking
of her own life. So, too, the death of his father and the betrayal of
his trust in his beloved mother by her early remarriage lead Hamlet into a state of profound melancholy in which he contemplates
suicide. But if the parallel situation serves to reveal how ultimate
are the twin evils of hypocrisy and death which Hamlet encounters,
evils of existence which might unhinge a lesser mind and lead it
to suicide, the fact that Hamlet finally holds a grip on his sanity
despite all his aberrations and rejects the possibility of suicide,
serves to enhance his moral stature.

Laertes' situation also parallels that of Hamlet. As a man, he immediately assumes the task of revenging his father's death, returns
to Denmark, gathers together a rabble army, overpowers the palace
and has the power to topple Claudius from his throne. The fact
that Laertes, without any claim to the throne, is so easily able to
gather sufficient power to gain the throne and destroy Claudius
shows how very easy it might have been for Hamlet to do the
same. For, as Claudius himself has twice said, Hamlet is "loved of
the distracted multitude" and Hamlet does have a legal claim to
the throne. But if Hamlet is guilty of procrastinating away all his
chances to revenge himself upon Claudius without also losing his
own life, the very fact that the mob will support someone like
Laertes, who has no royal pretensions, shows how anarchic and
illegitimate is such support. Laertes' attitude towards revenge serves,
moreover, to place Hamlet in a still brighter light. To accomplish
his revenge, Laertes is willing to give "vows to the blackest devil"
and to "dare damnation." Hamlet, however, has ever been disturbed
by the possibility that "The spirit that I have seen / May be a
devil . . . and perhaps / Out of weakness and my melancholy . . .
Abuses me to damn me." Though Hamlet may have other unfathomed psychological motives for not prosecuting his revenge, his perhaps
rationalized objection is a valid one and, in fact, he does not act
upon the ghost's evidence until he has first tested its validity through
the play within the play and then gained further evidence of Claudius' evil purposes. Even then he does not act to perform a personal

revenge which, whatever the truth of Claudius' crimes, might still damn Hamlet's own soul, finally transcending the motive of personal revenge altogether to judicially execute Claudius only for those public crimes, the poisoning of his mother and plotting of his own death, to which Laertes has confessed before the assembled court. If personal revenge, such as that which Laertes had attempted, might have damned his soul, the judicial execution which Hamlet finally does accomplish through his divine ministry not only scourges Denmark of its evils but serves to redeem his own soul.

The final minor character who enhances our respect for Hamlet is Horatio, who serves throughout as a model of moral righteousness. The fact that he always sides with Hamlet against Claudius, supporting his intentions even while attempting to restrain its excesses, serves to justify Hamlet's behavior. And it is Horatio who speaks the final eulogy over the dead body of Hamlet, words which remain with us as our final picture of Hamlet and voucher for his spiritual regeneration: "Now cracks a noble heart. Good night, sweet prince, / And flights of angels sing thee to thy rest!"

Q. 5: Why does the tragic conflict of Hamlet and Claudius, the "mighty opposites" of the play, leave so many other deaths in its wake and in what sense are these other characters responsible for their deaths?

A. 5: As Hamlet says in explaining his arrangements for the deaths of Rosencrantz and Guildenstern: " 'Tis dangerous when the baser nature comes / Between the pass and fell incensed points / Of mighty opposites." In the world of tragedy, the scourging of evil often involves a holocaust of those less corrupt natures which might have escaped tragedy were it not for the original wrenching of natural order achieved by the first crime, a wrenching which universal justice seeks to redress. In the process, many of those who have attached themselves to the original wrongdoer, especially if a king, are also scourged. As Rosencrantz explained: "The cease of majesty / Dies not alone, but, like a gulf doth draw / What's near it with it . . . Each small annexment, petty consequence, / Attends the boisterous ruin." But if "each small annexment" is destroyed in consequence of his involvement, each is also destroyed through the tragic testing of his own flaws of character, known in critical terms as the "tragic flaw."

The simplest examples of this process are Rosencrantz and Guildenstern who, as perfect courtiers, attach themselves to the King's welfare and will, obeying his orders without presuming to examine their nature. When this involves them, perhaps innocently, in carrying Claudius' orders for the execution of Hamlet, they become criminal accomplices of a criminal King and were liable to the punishment which Hamlet metes out to them.

A more complex example of the courtier who unfortunately attached himself to a king marked for destruction by universal justice is Polonius. And here it is not simply his attachment to Claudius' purposes but his own character flaw which accounts for his tragedy. For Polonius is an old presumptuous fool, who, feeling, perhaps rightly, that he has outlived his usefulness to the state, is overly anxious to prove his worth through that ability on which he most prides himself, his aptitude for spying. Having arranged one unsuccessful spying incident in which he watched with Claudius from behind a hanging tapestry the meeting between Hamlet and Ophelia, he is not content but busies himself to plan another confrontation between Hamlet and Gertrude which he also plans to watch from behind a tapestry. But his anxiety to prove his worth is also joined to a failing perception of human motivation, especially of one so complex as Hamlet. As he first misjudged Hamlet's intentions towards his daughter, ruining her happiness as well as increasing Hamlet's disillusionment with life by ordering her to reject his advances, so now he fatally misjudges the passionate involvement of Hamlet with his mother's sins, and the murderous outburst to which their meeting soon leads results in his own death.

As Polonius' destruction resulted from his dependence on the King, so Ophelia's destruction results from her dependence upon her father, Polonius. Raised by him to be completely dependent upon and obedient to his judgment, she rejects Hamlet, whom she loves, and allows herself to be used by her father in his spying attempt upon Hamlet, only to be abused by her lover. When her father is killed, however, she is unable to cope with reality on her own, and the combination of her father's death and lover's abuse serves to unhinge her mind and to cause her to lose her life. Her obedient dependence upon a corrupt support destroys her just as it did her father.

Another tragic result of Polonius' poor paternal tutelage is Laertes. Raised by his father to esteem the outward marks of honor more than its inner reality, he seeks to revenge his father's death primarily because the honor code demands it. His concern with the outward show of honor is particularly marked in his distress over the lack of formal ostentation in the funerals of his father and sister. But to accomplish the revenge which he believes honor to demand, he is willing to use the most dishonorable means. Attaching himself tragically to Claudius' own corrupt purposes, he agrees to engage in a practice fencing match with Hamlet, using an illegally sharpened and poisoned sword. When Hamlet offers him the possibility of honorable reconcilement, a possibility to which his nature responds, he says that he will honor Hamlet's offer, though he will not accept formal reconcilement until he can be shown precedents of such reconciliations which will prove that his honor will not be left spotted, and then proceeds to completely dishonor himself by betraying his pact with Hamlet and mortally wounding him after the fencing round is over. For this dishonorable behavior in the twisted pursuit of honor, he is himself destroyed by Hamlet. But he redeems his soul if not his life by his final movement from the side of Claudius to that of Hamlet, confessing Claudius' crimes before the court and exchanging forgiveness with Hamlet in his death.

The final tragic figure who moves from her attachment to Claudius to the side of Hamlet, though after she has been doomed to death, is Gertrude. And here again it is the tragic flaw in her character rather than the simple fact of her sinful attachment of Claudius which dooms her. Gertrude has always tried to avoid the sight of anything painful. This character flaw, which might have partially accounted for Claudius' need to murder her husband so that he could marry her and end what must have been a distressing liason to her, is revealed in the fact that she has not been able to bring herself to see Hamlet alone for two months after her marriage, and then only does so in the hope to avoid his exile, and in her desire to avoid seeing the insane Ophelia. What she desires more than anything is to see her two loves, Claudius and Hamlet, reconciled. When, during the duel, it appears that her dearest wish is to be achieved, that Hamlet has not only been reconciled with Laertes but has been willing to fight as Claudius' champion, she so deludes herself into believing that the catastrope she has long feared but tried to avoid facing has been stayed, that she actively joins into the happy occasion and drinks to Hamlet's good fortune. But the drink intended for Hamlet has been poisoned by Claudius, whose evil Gertrude has consistently refused to admit, and she dies a victim of her own foolish desire to avoid tragedy.

BIBLIOGRAPHY

I. TEXTUAL AND SOURCE STUDIES:

Duthie, G.I., *The "Bad" Quarto of Hamlet*. Cambridge, The University Press, 1941.

Gollancz, Sir Israel, *The Sources of Hamlet, With an Essay on the Legend*. London, Oxford University Press, 1926.

Greg, W.W., *The Editorial Problem in Shakespeare: A Survey of the Foundations of the Text*. Oxford, Clarendon Press, 1942.

II. EARLIER CRITICISM:

Coleridge, Samuel Taylor, *Coleridge's Shakespearean Criticism*. Thomas Middleton Raysor, ed. Cambridge, Harvard University Press, 1930.

Goethe, Johann Wolfgang von, *Wilhelm Meister's Apprenticeship* (1796), trans. Thomas Carlyle (1824). London, Chapman and Hall Ltd., n.d. (Vol. I, Book IV, Chapter XIII).

Johnson, Samuel, *Johnson on Shakespeare: Essays and Notes Selected and Set Forth with an Introduction by Walter Raleigh*. London, Oxford University Press, 1908.

III. TWENTIETH CENTURY CRITICISM:

Bradley, A.C., *Shakespearean Tragedy*. New York, Meridian Books, 1955. (1904)

Eliot, T.S., "Hamlet and His Problems" (1919), in *Selected Essays: 1917-1932*. New York, Harcourt, Brace and Company, 1932.

Elliot, G.R., *Scourge and Min.ster: A Study of Hamlet as Tragedy of Revengefulness and Justice*. Durham, N.C., Duke University Press, 1951.

Grebanier, Bernard, *The Heart of Hamlet: The Play Shakespeare Wrote*. New York, Thomas Y. Crowell Company, 1960.

Johnson, S.F., "The Regeneration of Hamlet," *Shakespeare Quarterly*, III (July, 1952).

Jones Ernest, *Hamlet and Oedipus*. New York, W.W. Norton & Company, 1949.

Kitto, H.D.F., *Form and Meaning in Drama*. London, Methuen and Company, 1956.

Knight, G. Wilson, "The Embassy of Death: An Essay on Hamlet," *The Wheel of Fire*. London, Oxford University Press, 1930.

Levin, Harry, *The Question of Hamlet*. New York, Oxford University Press, 1959.

Lewis, C.S., "Hamlet: The Prince or the Poem?" *Proceedings of the British Academy XXXVIII*. London, Oxford University Press, 1942.

Mack, Maynard, "The World of *Hamlet*," *Yale Review*, XLI (1952), 502-523.

Madariaga, Salvador de, *On Hamlet*. London, Hollis and Carter, 1948.

Miriam Joseph, Sister, C.S.C. "Hamlet, A Christian Tragedy," *Studies in Philology*, LIX (1962), 119-140.

Robertson, J.M., *The Problem of "Hamlet."* London, G. Allen & Unwin, 1919.

Spurgeon, Caroline, *Shakespeare's Imagery and What It Tells Us*. Boston, Beacon Press, 1958. (1935)

Stoll, E.E., *Hamlet: an Historical and Comparative Study*. Minneapolis, University of Minnesota Press, 1919.

Traversi, D.K., *An Approach to Shakespeare*. New York, Doubleday, 1956. (1936)

Van Doren, Mark, *Shakespeare*. New York, Doubleday, 1953. (1939)

Williamson, Claude C.H., *Readings in the Character of Hamlet: 1661-1947*. London, G. Allen and Unwin, 1950.

Wilson, Harold S., *On the Design of Shakespearean Tragedy*. Toronto, 1957.

Wilson, John Dover, *What Happens in Hamlet*. Cambridge, The University Press, 1962. (1935)

NOTES

NOTES

NOTES

NOTES

NOTES

MONARCH® NOTES AND STUDY GUIDES

ARE AVAILABLE AT RETAIL STORES EVERYWHERE

In the event your local bookseller cannot provide you with other Monarch titles you want —

ORDER ON THE FORM BELOW:

Complete order form appears on inside front & back covers for your convenience.

Simply send retail price, local sales tax, if any, plus 35¢ per book to cover mailing and handling.

TITLE #	AUTHOR & TITLE (exactly as shown on title listing)	PRICE
	PLUS ADDITIONAL 35¢ PER BOOK FOR POSTAGE	
	GRAND TOTAL	$

MONARCH® PRESS, a Simon & Schuster Division of Gulf & Western Corporation
Mail Service Department, 1230 Avenue of the Americas, New York, N.Y. 10020

I enclose $ .... to cover retail price, local sales tax, plus mailing and handling.

Name _____
(Please print)
Address _____

City _____ State _____ Zip _____

Please send check or money order. We cannot be responsible for cash.